THE ELDERCARE SOURCEBOOK

ANN RHODES

KEY PORTER BOOKS

The publisher gratefully acknowledges the assistance of the Canada Council and the Ontario Arts Council.

CANADIAN CATALOGING IN PUBLICATION DATA

Rhodes, Ann, 1932—
The eldercare sourcebook: a guide for caregivers

Includes bibliographical references and index.
ISBN 1-55013-475-2

1. Aged—Services for—Canada—Directories.
I. Title.

HV1450.R56 1993 362.6'0971 C93-094225-6

Key Porter Books Limited
70 The Esplanade
Toronto, Ontario
Canada M5E 1R2

Typesetting: True to Type
Printed and bound in Canada
93 94 95 96 6 5 4 3 2 1

CONTENTS

ACKNOWLEDGEMENTS

FIRST OF ALL, I WOULD LIKE TO THANK ALL THOSE WHO took the time to give interviews, send in material, or otherwise help in the task of collecting and collating information about services and programs for older Canadians from coast to coast. They are too numerous to name here, but they will know who they are.

Many of them are on the staff of the federal and provincial governmental departments concerned with aging and elders, and many others are on the staff of the organizations named in this book. These latter groups were especially helpful, and I have great admiration for the professionalism and caring attitudes they bring to their work.

I would like to thank the publisher and editors at Key Porter Books, both for giving me the chance to write this book and also for giving me encouragement along the way. Here again, I encountered a high degree of professionalism.

Finally, my very special thanks to my research colleague Jerri Yeomans. She brought in a remarkable volume of information in a relatively short space of time. And, no less importantly, she helped greatly in devising the structure of the book at the outset and keeping it on track along the way.

Ann Rhodes
August 1993

INTRODUCTION

THE NEED FOR A BOOK OF THIS NATURE IS LARGE NOW, and will almost certainly grow exponentially over the next decades for several reasons.

First, the greying of a large proportion of Canada's population—and, indeed, that of the entire Western world—has already begun. According to the National Advisory Council on Aging, while those aged 65 or older made up 9.7 per cent of Canada's population in 1981, the proportion had grown to 10.7 per cent by 1986, and 11.6 per cent by 1991. By 2021, according to one estimate, one in five Canadians—that's a whopping 20 per cent of the population— will be 65 or older. In short, as elderly Canadians increase in number, so do caregivers needing to know where to turn for help.

Second, life expectancy of Canadians is increasing: women can now expect to live to age 80, up from 74 in the early 1960s, and men to age 73, up from 68 over the same period. This trend also leads inevitably to more elders, and more needy caregivers.

This book is designed primarily to help elders and their caregivers plan in such a way that elders can remain in the community at large, rather than going into permanent institutional care of some kind. Most elders want to remain in the community (cases in which they want to go into permanent care because they are lonely or afraid of living alone are relatively rare). And this is something all of us, and not just elders, should want. Aside from quality-of-life issues, keeping someone in permanent care can cost up to $350 a day—money that, in the final analysis, comes out of all our pockets in the form of tax dollars. By contrast, using appropriate services and programs, a caregiver may be able to help an elder remain at home for as little as $50 a week.

Our society "warehouses" too many elders instead of working to keep them in the community, and in so doing robs itself of a font of matchless wisdom and experience. Of Canadians aged 65 and older, 7.5 per cent were in permanent care in 1990, according to the National Advisory Council on Aging. Only the Netherlands, at 11 per cent, had a larger institutionalization rate for those aged 65 or older. Proportions for some other countries, for the purpose of comparison, were: Austria, 6.8 per cent; the United States, 4.6 per cent; West Germany (these statistics were compiled before unification), 4.5 per cent; and Great Britain, 4.1 per cent. Ontario, with 7.5 per cent of those aged 65 to

74 and 15 per cent of those aged 75 or older in permanent care, has the world's highest rate of institutionalization, according to the Senior Citizens' Consumer Alliance for Long-Care Reform.

Many caregivers, seven out of ten of whom are women, are members of what has become known as the Sandwich Generation: in other words, they already give care to children who have not yet left home, and are now starting to give care to parents or other elderly relatives. Many of them also hold down full-time jobs, and so are triply stressed. If they don't get outside help of some kind, they run a real risk of becoming ill themselves.

The core problem is that many caregivers don't know which doors to knock on to find the specific forms of help they need. Indeed, many don't even know where the doors are. (I have been in such a situation and know all too well the frustrating feeling of knowing help is needed and being unable to find it.) As a consequence, caregivers or their elders, or both, decide that the only way out of an impossibly trying situation is for the elders to go into permanent care.

A huge volume, or perhaps several volumes, would be needed to list all the services and programs available for elders right across the country. But I hope that this book will at least point caregivers in the right directions by indicating the most important doors, to continue the analogy. More often than not, once the right door has been opened and the seeker is inside the system at last, other doors also open.

Efforts to keep this volume at a manageable size, and therefore affordable, have meant that not every program and service coast to coast is included. Because a certain program or service is listed for a particular centre, region, or province only does not mean it exists nowhere else. Ask around: you may well find that a service or program listed for another area is available in your area too.

You will by now have noticed the use of the word "elder" instead of "senior." We have adopted the former for two reasons. Many older people dislike the term "senior." And my colleagues and I prefer "elder," which has the connotation of "elders and betters," since many older people are far more resilient and stronger in spirit than those of us who came along in later generations.

If you flip to the back of the book, you will find blank pages bearing the title "My Sources." These have been provided to help you to keep track of addresses and telephone numbers of local branches of organizations, and names and numbers of contact personnel. (In some sections, space restrictions have mandated against our listing full addresses. Instead, we have identified centres in which organizations are located, so that you can look up the addresses in your telephone directory.)

A second edition of *The Eldercare Sourcebook* may be compiled and published in two or three years. It can become, in a real sense, your book. If you know of valuable services or programs for elders that do not appear in this edition, please let us know by writing to Eldercare Sources, Key Porter Books Limited, 70 The Esplanade, Toronto, Ontario M5E 1R2.

CHAPTER ONE

OPENING THE FIRST DOOR

AS WE MENTIONED IN THE INTRODUCTION, ONCE YOU have located and opened the first door and entered the system, other doors are likely to open speedily. You have several choices of a "first door," all of them close at hand.

One is your elder's family physician. She or he will probably know what services and programs are available for elders in the community. Go together to ask.

Another is a public health nurse, who will certainly know what is available locally. To find a public health nurse, look in the blue pages of your telephone directory, where you will find a listing for "Health Care Services," "Health Services," or "Public Health Services" in the municipal government section. A nurse may give you the information you need over the telephone, or may come to your home to advise you about the programs and services that exist in your community, and to give general counsel if it is needed.

Yet another "first door" is that of your local community information centre. Such centres exist right across the country, even in smaller communities, and are a rich source of information about local programs and services. In some places, they are not called community information centres; ask staff at the health department or your local library to help you locate one in your community—or that of your elder if he or she does not live in your community. In Quebec, these centres are often called information and referral centres.

The Association of Community Information Centres in Ontario (ACICO) has a listing of centres, not only in Ontario but also in Alberta, British Columbia, and Quebec. Contact the ACICO at 5233 Dundas Street West, Suite 205, Etobicoke, Ontario M9B 1A6.

Another choice of "first door" is your local branch of the Victorian Order of Nurses. VON personnel are highly knowledgeable regarding programs and service for elders, and will gladly share their knowledge with you. Check your telephone directory for your local branch.

Or you might contact your local family service association. Family service associations—in some places called family services, family centres, family counselling centres, or family life bureaus—exist right across the country, providing numerous services for families and family members, including elders, couples, and children. In many cases, they have support programs for elders and caregivers, offering all kinds of counsel, whether it be on services in the community or information about retirement homes and other types of living accommodations in the area. To find out the name and location of the organization nearest to you, contact Family Service Canada, 55 Parkdale Avenue, Ottawa, Ontario K1Y 4G1.

Or you might ask a senior librarian at your local library. Librarians are often well-informed about programs and services in the community.

In several provinces, there is already only one "door." And this will also be the case in Ontario in the next few years.

New Brunswick has a single entry point program. You call the nearest office of the New Brunswick Extra-Mural Hospital (hospital without walls), and an extra-mural nurse and a social worker come to the home to assess an elder's needs and to determine if home care will be sufficient and, if so, what kind. If the client should be in permanent care, they determine at what level. Single entry point staff put in place whatever services clients need. They also check regularly to find out whether clients' needs are still being met.

In Alberta, the single entry point is the Health Unit in your community. In British Columbia it is your local Health Unit or Health Department, in Manitoba the nearest regional office of Manitoba Health and Family Services, and in Saskatchewan the community Homecare office.

Ontario already has Placement Co-ordination Services (PCSs) in some areas. Clients of PCSs are those who need permanent care. PCS staff determine what level of care is needed and direct clients to an appropriate long-term care facility. Over the next few years Multi-Service Agencies (MSAs) will be introduced. MSAs will be staffed by specialists in all types of home care and PCS personnel. Thus MSA assessors will recommend eldercare ranging from the most basic home services all the way up to long-term care placement.

CHAPTER TWO

WHAT IS GOING ON HERE?

ONCE, AN ASTUTE SOCIAL WORKER OBSERVED THAT family members often fail to diagnose elders' problems correctly, mistaking minor difficulties for major ones. This is a cheering thought. Nevertheless, how can you be sure? Perhaps the elder you care for seems to have gone downhill quite severely. She or he could have a major problem. What do you do?

Your first call should probably be to the elder's family physician—with the elder's knowledge. (Do not go behind his or her back: would you want someone to do that to you?) The physician may be able to reassure you that the problem is not severe. Or, if examination reveals the likelihood of a major problem, the physician may refer the elder to a geriatric assessment unit (GAU), both to arrive at a complete diagnosis of the elder's physical state and social environment and to recommend a course of action.

GAUs are a relatively recent development in the field of geriatrics. A unit is a team, working under the aegis of a hospital or health care centre. Team composition varies, but some or all of the following may be involved: physiotherapist, social worker, dietitian, occupational therapist, pharmacist, gerontological nurse, and physician.

More often than not, the elder is interviewed and examined by team members at the hospital, but a visit to the home will also be scheduled, for example, for the occupational therapist to find out whether it is suitable or needs some modification in the light of the elder's disability. However, if for whatever reason an elder cannot go to the hospital, the team will visit her or him in the home. Family members will almost certainly also be interviewed, in order to collect various kinds of information and to build up a picture of the elder's social environment.

In almost all cases, referrals to a GAU are made by a family physician, another health care professional, or a social worker. Sometimes, caregivers contact a GAU directly, but such action should not be taken. Given the number of professionals and the amount of time involved in making an assessment, a direct contact by a caregiver who mistakes a minor problem for a major one is an expensive misuse of a valuable resource. (The cost to you is nil, however; provincial health care plans pick up the tab for assessments.)

Want to know whether there is a GAU near you? (Almost certainly there is: they are proliferating fast.

Whereas three years ago there were just over 100 in existence, at the time of writing, there were more than 160.) Turn to the end of this chapter, where you'll find an alphabetical listing of GAUs by province, taken from the appendix to *Geriatric Assessment and Treatment: Members of the Team*, a publication compiled by and available without charge from the National Advisory Council on Aging (NACA), 473 Albert Street, Ottawa, Ontario K1A 0K9.

Members of the Victorian Order of Nurses also do assessments, whose cost is again covered by provincial health care plans. Contact the head office of VON Canada at 5 Blackburn Avenue, Ottawa, Ontario K1N 8A2, or your local branch.

Public health nurses make assessments as well. Again, there is no charge; the municipality picks up the tab. As you learned in Chapter 1, to contact a public health nurse, look in the blue pages of your telephone directory, where you'll almost certainly find "Health Care Services," "Health Services," or "Public Health Services" in the municipal government listings.

Occupational therapists (OTs) can assess an elder's physical environment to determine whether it is appropriate or needs modification in order that the occupant may function safely and comfortably there. However, they are not qualified to assess the occupant's state of health.

If a physician or health care professional makes a referral, an OT's fee for assessing a home is usually covered by a home care or hospital budget. If a caregiver or an elder hires an OT directly, without a referral, he or she will pay a fee. If the user has private health care insurance, it may cover the fee; check with the insurer before approaching an OT, since some private policies require a referral from a physician before paying an OT's fee.

OTs are listed in the Yellow Pages for some locations. If they are not listed in yours, you might ask the family physician or the information desk at the local hospital for names. Or write to the Canadian Association of Occupational Therapists at 110 Eglinton Avenue West, 3rd Floor, Toronto, Ontario M4R 1A3.

The hospitals and health care centres listed below operate geriatric assessment services.

Alberta

Athabasca: Athabasca General & Auxiliary Hospital
Black Diamond: Oilfields General Hospital
Blairmore: Crowsnest Pass Health Care Centre
Calgary: Bethany Care Centre, Calgary General Hospital, Care West, Colonel Belcher Hospital, University of Calgary Health Science Centre
Cardston: Municipal Auxiliary Hospital
Coaldale: Coaldale Health Care Centre
Cold Lake: Cold Lake Regional Hospital

Coronation: Coronation Paintearth Auxiliary Hospital & Nursing Home

Drayton Valley: Drayton Valley & District Health Complex

Drumheller: Drumheller Regional Health Complex

Edmonton: Alberta Hospital, Glenrose Rehabilitation Hospital, Good Samaritan Auxiliary Hospital, Royal Alexandra Hospital, Youville Geriatric Services at Edmonton General Hospital

Grande Prairie: Queen Elizabeth II Hospital

Innisfail: Innisfail Health Care

Ponoka: Alberta Hospital, Ponoka General Hospital

Rocky Mountain House: Rocky Mountain House General and Auxiliary Hospital

Taber: Taber and District Health Care Complex

Vegreville: St. Joseph's General Hospital, Vegreville Auxiliary Hospital and Nursing Home

British Columbia

Abbotsford: Matsqui-Sumas-Abbotsford General Hospital

Chemainus: Chemainus Hospital

Port Coquitlam: Riverview Hospital

Vancouver: Holy Family Hospital, Mt. Saint Joseph's Hospital, Vancouver General Hospital, St. Paul's Hospital, University Hospital (Shaughnessy Site)

Victoria: Fairfield Health Centre, Greater Victoria Hospital Society, Juan de Fuca Hospital Society

Manitoba

Brandon: Brandon Mental Health Centre
Melita: Melita Health Centre
Portage La Prairie: Portage District General Hospital
Winkler: Eden Mental Health Centre
Winnipeg: Deer Lodge Centre Inc., Health Sciences Centre, Seven Oaks General Hospital, St. Boniface General Hospital, Winnipeg Municipal Hospital

New Brunswick

Bathurst: Chaleur Regional Hospital
Edmundston: Edmundston Regional Hospital
Moncton: The Moncton Hospital
Oromocto: Oromocto Public Hospital
Saint John: Saint John Regional Hospital

Newfoundland

Corner Brook: Western Memorial Hospital
St. John's: The Leonard A. Miller Centre for Health Services, The Salvation Army Grace General Hospital, Waterford Hospital

Nova Scotia

Antigonish: St. Martha's Hospital
Dartmouth: The Nova Scotia Hospital
Halifax: Camp Hill Hospital

Ontario

Atikokan: Atikokan General Hospital
Burlington: Joseph Brant Memorial Hospital
Cambridge: Cambridge Memorial Hospital
Carleton: Almonte General Hospital
Chatham: Public General Hospital
Etobicoke: Queensway General Hospital
Fort Frances: Laverendrye General Hospital
Hamilton: Chedoke-McMaster Hospital, St. Joseph's Hospital, St. Peter's Hospital
Hawkesbury: Hawkesbury General Hospital
Kingston: St. Mary's of the Lake Hospital
Kitchener: The Freeport Hospital
London: Parkwood Hospital, St. Joseph's Health Centre of London
Mississauga: The Mississauga Hospital
Niagara Falls: Greater Niagara General Hospital
North York: North York General Hospital
Ottawa: Elisabeth Bruyère Health Centre, Montford Hospital, National Defence Medical Centre, Ottawa Civic Hospital, Ottawa General Hospital, Queensway-Carleton Hospital, St. Vincent Hospital
Owen Sound: Grey-Bruce Regional Health Centre
Pembroke: Pembroke General Hospital
Penetanguishene: Penetanguishene General Hospital
Sarnia: Sarnia General Hospital, St. Joseph Hospital
Scarborough: Centenary Health Centre, Providence

Centre, Scarborough General Hospital, West Park Hospital
Smiths Falls: Smiths Falls Community Hospital (South Unit)
Sudbury: Laurentian Hospital
Toronto: The Queen Elizabeth Hospital, Runnymede Hospital, St. Michael's Hospital, Sunnybrook Medical Centre
Weston: Humber Memorial Hospital
Whitby: Whitby General Hospital
Williamsburg: Sydenham District Hospital
Windsor: Windsor Western Hospital Centre

Prince Edward Island
Charlottetown: Queen Elizabeth Hospital

Quebec
Amqui: Amqui Hospital
Arthabaska: Hôtel-Dieu d'Arthabaska Hospital
Asbestos: Asbestos Hospital
Beauport: Robert-Giffard Hospital, Roy-Rousseau Clinic, St-Augustin Hospital
Charny: Paul-Gilbert Hospital
Drummondville: Centre hospitalier Georges Frédéric, Sainte Croix Hospital
Fleurimont: Sherbrooke University Hospital
Granby: Granby Hospital

Hull: Outaouais Regional Hospital, Pieta Hospital
Jonquière: Jonquière Hospital
Kahnawake: Kaleri Hospital
Lachine: Lachine Hospital
Lachute: Argenteuil Hospital
Laval: Laval St-Jude Hospital
Longueuil: Pierre Boucher Hospital
Megantic Lake: Megantic Lake Hospital
Mont-Laurier: Mont-Laurier Hospital
Montmagny: Hôtel-Dieu de Montmagny Hospital
Montreal: Côte-des-Neiges Hospital, Hôtel-Dieu de Montréal Hospital, Jacques-Viger Hospital, Jean-Talon Hospital, Jewish General Hospital, JH-Charbonneau Hospital, Maimonides Hospital, Maisonneuve-Rosemont Hospital, Notre-Dame Hospital, Notre-Dame de la Merci Hospital, Queen Elizabeth Montreal Hospital, Royal Victoria Hospital, Sacré-Coeur Montreal Hospital, St-Luc Hospital, St. Mary's Hospital Centre
Quebec City: Centre hospitalier de l'Université Laval, Courchesne Hospital, Hôtel-Dieu de Québec, L'Enfant Jésus Hospital, Quebec General Hospital, St-François d'Assise Hospital, St-Sacrement Hospital
Rivière-du-Loup: Regional Grand-Portage Hospital
Roberval: Hôtel-Dieu de Roberval Hospital
Sainte Anne De Bellevue: Ste. Anne Hospital
Ste-Foy: Laval University Hospital
St-Hyacinthe: Hôtel-Dieu de St-Hyacinthe

St-Jean: Haut-Richelieu Hospital
St-Jérôme: Hôtel-Dieu de Saint-Jérôme Hospital, Youville Hospital
St-Lambert: St-Lambert Hospital
Sherbrooke: D'Youville Hospital, Hôtel-Dieu Hospital, St-Vincent de Paul Hospital
Thetford Mines: General Hospital of la Région de l'Amiante Inc.
Trois-Rivières: Cooke Hospital
Valleyfield: Valleyfield Hospital
Verdun: Champlain de Verdun Hospital, Douglas Hospital
Vimont: Cité de la Santé de Laval
Windsor: St-Louis de Windsor Hospital

Saskatchewan
Bienfait: Bienfait Coalfields Union Hospital
Estevan: St. Joseph Hospital
Kerrabert: Kerrabert Union Hospital
Melville: St. Peter Hospital
Regina: Regina General Hospital

CHAPTER THREE

HELPING HANDS

IN RECENT YEARS, THE NUMBER OF BOTH PUBLIC AND private homecare services has grown—not surprisingly, given the greying of the population. Just look in your Yellow Pages under "Nursing" and see how many entries you find.

A wide variety of options to choose from may sound like good news. But unless you know what categories of help are available to your elder and what kind of service will best fill his or her needs, choice can also be confusing.

It helps to know, first, that there are, broadly speaking, three categories of homecare services—public, non-profit, and commercial. And, as you'll discover shortly, available help ranges all the way from occasional light housekeeping to specialized nursing services, such as intravenous therapy and even chemotherapy.

PUBLIC SERVICES

To find public (i.e., government operated) homemaking

and health care services of all kinds, contact a public health nurse. (You learned how to find a public health nurse in Chapter 1.)

Your family physician may also be knowledgeable about public services available in the community. So may your local family service association and community information centre. (You also learned how to locate a family service association and a community information centre in your area in Chapter 1.)

Public services cover both homemaking and health care. Offerings include housekeeping and yard help; general health counselling; meal preparation and/or delivery; nursing; care of feet, skin, and hair; assistance with such activities as bathing, dressing, and taking medications; specialized care for specific conditions such as diabetes or arthritis; and occupational therapy, physiotherapy, and speech therapy.

If you and your elder feel you need a public service, ask the family physician or the public health nurse for a referral. The care receiver will pay no fees unless she or he continues to use the service for a longer period than that specified by the doctor or nurse. Even then, fees are on a sliding scale, so no users pay more than they can afford.

NON-PROFIT SERVICES

Non-profit services typically set fees on a sliding scale,

often with stated minimums and maximums, so clients are not charged more than they can afford to pay. As well, if users are covered by a provincial health care plan, Blue Cross Extended Care, veterans' benefits, or any other type of health insurance, the cost of these services may be covered.

Your family physician or local family service association and community information centre can probably direct you to non-profit services in the area.

Here's a brief rundown of three non-profit organizations that provide services at several locations.

VON Canada

With more than 70 branches across the country and more than 6,000 staff members and 10,000 volunteers, the Victorian Order of Nurses is Canada's largest provider of home health care. VON Canada workers offer nursing services, respiratory care, and palliative care (for patients who are not expected to live). They perform enterostomal (post-surgical fitting of a patient with an internal or external pouch for waste excretion) and intravenous therapy, and provide meals on wheels, volunteer visiting, and counselling on rehabilitation, diet, and exercise. They also teach elders how to take care of their feet.

In the quick response program, VON staff assess elders brought to the emergency department of a hospital. If admission to the hospital proves not to be necessary, they provide the kind of care needed in the home.

The VON's respite workers assume the duties of the family caregiver in the home so that the caregiver has a regular routine of time off—perhaps a few afternoons, or a weekend away, or a short vacation. (Another way of providing respite for caregivers is for elders to spend time at a VON adult day care centre.) They also teach caregivers how to make their role easier. In a few areas, they provide homemaking services such as grocery shopping, planning and preparing meals, and light housekeeping.

There are two ways in which to get assistance from the VON: call your local branch direct, or discuss your elder's needs with her or his physician and ask the physician to call the VON or to refer your elder to the organization. If you call direct, VON personnel will ask about your needs and then call the physician to confirm the elder's condition and discuss requirements.

The head office of VON Canada is at 5 Blackburn Avenue, Ottawa, Ontario K1N 8A2. The organization has the following branches:

Alberta

Calgary, Edmonton, Grande Prairie and Region, Lethbridge, Medicine Hat and District

British Columbia
Richmond-Vancouver
Manitoba
Winnipeg
New Brunswick
Bathurst, Campbellton, Edmundston, Fredericton, Miramichi, Moncton, Oromocto, Sackville, Saint John, Woodstock
Newfoundland
Corner Brook, St. John's
Ontario
Brant-Norfolk-Haldimand, Brockville, Chatham-Kent, Durham Region, Eastern Counties, Eastern Lake Ontario, Guelph-Wellington-Dufferin, Grey Bruce, Halton, Hamilton-Wentworth, Kirkland Lake, Lanark, Middlesex-Elgin, Metropolitan Toronto, Niagara, North Bay, Ottawa-Carleton, Oxford, Peel, Pembroke, Perth-Huron, Peterborough-Victoria-Haliburton, Porcupine, Quinte, Sarnia-Lambton, Sault Ste. Marie, Simcoe County, South Renfrew, Sudbury, Thunder Bay and District, Waterloo County, Windsor-Essex, York
Quebec
Hudson, Lachine-Dorval, Montreal, Ste. Anne's and District
Saskatchewan
Moose Jaw, Prince Albert, Regina, Saskatoon

The Canadian Red Cross Society

Of the society's 550 branches across Canada, 59 provide homecare services; check with your local branch to find out whether it is one of the 59.

Red Cross homecare personnel provide bedside care and assistance with bathing, dressing, grooming, toileting, and feeding. They provide respite care so that caregivers can take a break. They assist people who have problems walking and those who need help to exercise regularly; they also accompany clients to appointments, and do home management chores, such as grocery shopping, meal planning and preparation (including special diets), light housekeeping, and laundry and ironing.

As well, the society runs meals on wheels and transportation services, friendly visiting programs, and Fun & Fitness classes. (For more information about these classes, see Chapter 10.)

For more information about the Canadian Red Cross Society, contact your local branch or write to the head office at 1800 Alta Vista Drive, Ottawa, Ontario K1G 4J5.

St. Elizabeth Visiting Nurses Association

The St. Elizabeth Visiting Nurses Association of Ontario has branches in Metro Toronto and in Peel and Durham regions. If a client is referred to the association by a municipal homecare program, the program will pay the association's fees. If a client goes directly to the association to obtain help, the client will be billed. But, as always, health insurance plans may cover the costs. As well, in some circumstances, if an elder cannot afford the fees, the association will make no charge.

To handle direct requests for help, the association maintains a registry of nurses. Those on the registry are located throughout Ontario.

The association employs about 500 nursing and administrative staff. Registered Nurses (RNs) and Registered Nurses' Aides (RNAs) provide service on an around-the-clock basis, seven days a week. Services include comprehensive health assessment, case management, health promotion, and assistance with specific health problems.

Among specialty services performed are private duty nursing; homemaking; foot care; general care for elders; respiratory monitoring; enterostomal therapy; mental health care; palliative care; and intravenous therapy, including chemotherapy.

The association's head office is located at 10 Gateway Boulevard, Don Mills, Ontario M3C 1A1.

COMMERCIAL SERVICES

Numerous commercial services are available. However, since these are not non-profit organizations, fees are set and will not be reduced or waived. Once again, however, users' health insurance will cover all or part of the cost.

Many private nursing services are one-location organizations, as you will realize when you examine advertisements in the Yellow Pages under the heading "Nursing." Others are multi-branch organizations. Some of the latter are discussed briefly below.

Olsten Healthcare

With 22 branches across Canada, Olsten is a large home health care provider. Its employees span a wide range of professions: registered, licensed, and vocational nurses; home health aides; homemakers; companions; physical and occupational therapists; speech pathologists; and medical social workers, among others.

Olsten Healthcare's head office is located at 111 Gordon Baker Road, Suite 420, North York, Ontario M2H 3R1. Branches are located in the following centres:

Alberta
Calgary, Edmonton
British Columbia
Burnaby, Coquitlam, Vancouver, Victoria
Manitoba
Winnipeg
New Brunswick
Fredericton, Moncton, Saint John
Newfoundland
Grand Falls, St. John's
Nova Scotia
Halifax

Ontario

Hamilton, London, Ottawa, St. Catharines, Thunder Bay, Toronto

Quebec

Montreal East, Montreal West, Quebec City

Para-Med Health Services

Para-Med is a division of Extendicare, which operates more than 200 long-term care facilities for elders. (For more information on Extendicare, see Chapter 9.)

Specialists on staff include nurses, therapists, attendants, and home support workers. They provide service to clients on an around-the-clock basis, seven days a week, if necessary. Among services provided are health assessments; private duty nursing; occupational health nursing; palliative care; and occupational therapy, physiotherapy and speech therapy. Many branches have teams that specialize in care for special problems, such as those who offer Alzheimer care, palliative care, psychiatric care, and rehabilitation.

Para-Med's head office is located at 3000 Steeles Avenue East, Suite 700, Markham, Ontario L3R 9W2. Branches are located in the following centres:

Alberta

Calgary, Edmonton

British Columbia

Abbotsford, Burnaby, Coquitlam, Nanaimo, North Vancouver, Prince George, Richmond, Vancouver, Victoria

Ontario

Bancroft, Barrie, Belleville, Brockville, Casselman, Chatham, Cornwall, Durham, Goderich, Guelph, Hamilton, Hawkesbury, Kanata, Kingston, Kitchener/Cambridge, Leamington, Lindsay, Listowel, London, Napanee, Newmarket, Niagara Falls, Oakville, Orleans, Oshawa, Ottawa, Parry Sound, Pembroke, Perth, Renfrew, St. Catharines, Sarnia, Scarborough, Stratford, Strathroy, Tillsonburg, Toronto, Walkerton, Winchester, Windsor

Comcare (Canada) Limited

Another large-scale provider of home care, Comcare (Canada) Limited offers a wide variety of services. Homemaker services include meal preparation, laundry, and housework. Health care services include nursing by RNs and RNAs, foot care, physiotherapy, occupational therapy, companion care sitting, respite care to give relief to family members, intravenous therapy, palliative care, and bereavement follow-up.

Comcare's head office is located at 18 Spadina Road, Toronto, Ontario M5R 2S7. Branches are located in the following centres:

Alberta

Calgary, Edmonton

British Columbia

Abbotsford, New Westminster, Surrey, Vancouver

New Brunswick

Fredericton, Moncton, Saint John

Newfoundland
St. John's
Nova Scotia
Halifax
Ontario
Belleville-Napanee-Gananoque, Brampton, Burlington, Guelph, Hamilton, Kingston, Kitchener, London, Mississauga, Newmarket/Richmond Hill/Thornhill, Niagara Falls, Oshawa, Ottawa, Sarnia, Scarborough, St. Catharines, Stratford, St. Thomas, Simcoe, Thunder Bay, Toronto, Windsor, Woodstock

Central Health Services

Central Health Services is a division of Central Park Lodges, which operates long-term care facilities for elders. (For more information on Central Park Lodges, see Chapter 9.) The organization provides home health care, ranging from light housekeeping to skilled professional care administered by trained nurses and therapists.

Its head office is located at 1120 Finch Avenue West, Suite 800, Downsview, Ontario M3J 3H7. It has branches in Montreal, Ottawa, Toronto, and Winnipeg.

Selectacare

Selectacare branch operators are all registered nurses with backgrounds in community health. Among services performed by Selectacare personnel are professional nursing care; help with personal care, shopping, meals, and laundry; help with small repairs and home maintenance; hairdressing; telephone monitoring (prearranged calls at a specified time to ensure the client is all right); driver escort and assistance with appointments and shopping; outings (maybe a meal or a theatre visit with several other congenial people); and health care planning for the future. Offices also have an emergency number which clients can call to receive an immediate response from the coordinator on duty.

Some home health care and nursing services will send personnel into a home for a minimum number of hours—three or four, perhaps. Selectacare will send in personnel for as much or as little time as is needed—for example, an hour a week just to make sure a client is in good health, is not in need of help with housework, and has plenty of food in the home.

Selectacare's head office is located at 139 Sheppard Avenue East, Willowdale, Ontario M2N 3A6. Branches are located in Vancouver and Winnipeg, and in Brampton, Burlington, Metro Toronto, Oakville, and Ottawa, Ontario.

DAYTIME CARE

An alternative to home care is daytime care. Here the elders come to the helpers, rather than vice versa. For instance, congregate dining (or wheels to meals, as it is sometimes called) is the flip side of meals on wheels.

Whereas meals on wheels brings food to the home, congregate dining brings transportation to the home so that the participant can go to the place where the food is being served.

Daytime care for elderly people can be public (government run), non-profit, or commercial. Those in day programs are typically picked up at their homes in the morning, have lunch at the centre where the program is being held, and are returned to their homes mid- to late afternoon.

Daytime care usually gives participants a chance to join in discussions, do exercises, play games, and perhaps take part in some specialized activity, such as arts and crafts. Sometimes those in day programs go on outings in groups.

Some daytime care programs also include specialized help. For instance, VON Canada runs many daytime care centres at which participants can have their blood pressure and blood sugar levels checked, and have foot care as well.

Some daytime care programs are specialized; for instance, programs exist in some places for those with Alzheimer's and for those with Parkinson's disease.

Unlike daytime care centres, which feature little or no medical care, day hospital programs are for people who do need some help or at least checkups for medical conditions. Although few people attend day hospital programs on a regular basis, as with daytime care patients usually are picked up in the morning and returned to their homes in the afternoon. While at the hospital, they may receive treatment from podiatrists, dentists, otolaryngologists (ear, nose, and throat specialists), or opthalmologists, for instance. Psychiatric day hospital programs, as their name suggests, provide therapy for patients with psychiatric problems.

To find daytime care programs, ask any or all of the following: the family physician, a public health nurse, staff at the community information centre, staff at a public library, and/or patrons of seniors' clubs. You might also ask at hospitals and retirement homes in the district: daytime care programs and day hospital programs are quite commonly run in such facilities.

FINAL THOUGHTS ON THE TOPIC

All the professional qualifications in the world are worth little unless those possessing them deliver services, of whatever kind, with compassion and good humour. Would you want someone to slap a plate of food down in front of you and say, "There you are then. That's your lot for today, like it or lump it." Would you want to be told, "You mean you've forgotten those exercises you do to strengthen your wrists? Lordy, you are losing your marbles, aren't you?" Elders deserve better than this.

So ask around. Canvass friends, acquaintances, and any other people in the community whom you know to be caregivers and whose elders have help of one kind or another. Especially when it comes to private home nursing services, you have many from which to choose, and both you and your care receiver will be happy knowing that the service you hire is staffed by people who do their jobs with humanity as well as skill.

If the elder you care for needs specialized help for a particular condition—arthritis or diabetes, perhaps—Chapter 4 tells you where to find such help.

CHAPTER FOUR

SPECIALIZED HELPING HANDS

ALL THE ORGANIZATIONS LISTED IN THIS CHAPTER provide direct support and assistance to elders—and, in some cases, younger people—with specific physiological or psychological problems. Many also provide help at a distance by raising funds for research into causes and treatments of diseases.

Some of these organizations have a single head office, and no local branches; others have a national head office, provincial head offices, and numerous local offices. In these latter cases, look first in your local telephone directory to see if there is a branch in the community. If there is not, contact your provincial head office to find out where the nearest branch is. We have provided addresses of both single and national head offices below, and have listed the centres in which provincial head offices are located.

In at least one other case, there is no national organization, and regional or provincial organizations are autonomous. They may not have the same name, but essentially they serve the same purpose.

The Alzheimer Society of Canada, 1320 Yonge Street, Suite 201, Toronto, Ontario M4T 1X2. Provincial head offices are located in: Alberta (Calgary), British Columbia (Vancouver), Manitoba (Winnipeg), New Brunswick (Fredericton), Newfoundland (St. John's), Nova Scotia (Halifax), Ontario (Toronto), Prince Edward Island (Charlottetown), Quebec (Montreal), and Saskatchewan (Regina). The society also has many local branches. It provides information, mostly in the form of handbooks, leaflets, and videos, about the disease, how to live with it on a daily basis, how caregivers can help, and where to get outside help. Individual members and groups with experience of Alzheimer's disease offer counsel and advice to those in need. The society also conducts ongoing research into potential causes, treatments, and—ultimately, it is hoped—a cure.

The Arthritis Society, 250 Bloor Street East, Suite 901, Toronto, Ontario M4W 3P2. Provincial and territorial head offices are located in Alberta and Northwest Territories (Calgary), British Columbia and Yukon (Vancouver), Manitoba (Winnipeg), New Brunswick (Fredericton), Newfoundland (c/o Nova Scotia division), Nova Scotia (Halifax), Ontario (Toronto), Prince Edward Island (c/o Nova Scotia division), Quebec

(Montreal), and Saskatchewan (Regina). The society has more than a thousand branches and tens of thousands of volunteers. It provides ongoing funding for research into the causes of and potential cures for arthritis, and also supports the medical education of arthritis specialists. It publishes a variety of educational materials, including information pamphlets that provide, among other things, details about arthritis medications and coping strategies for daily living. It also publishes *Arthritis News*, a quarterly magazine about arthritis (see Chapter 13). Its arthritis self-management program is designed to give participants a sense of control over their arthritis. The society also assists in the formation of self-help support groups. In some provinces, it runs treatment programs for those with arthritis. As well, it sponsors seminars and public forums.

The Back Association of Canada, 83 Cottingham Street, Toronto, Ontario M4V 1B9. The association prepares and distributes information about back care in order that those with back pain can make informed decisions in choosing preventive action and treatment. It disseminates printed information in the form of leaflets, and a quarterly journal, *Back to Back* (see Chapter 13). It counsels its members on good back care, and encourages schools to teach good back care, and commerce and industry to provide goods, services, and working environments conducive to good back care.

The Bob Rumball Centre for the Deaf, 2395 Bayview Avenue, North York, Ontario M2L 1A2. The centre runs classes in sign language, communications skills, life skills management, math skills, English-language comprehension and written skills, and emotional training for hearing-impaired adults. Hearing-impaired people aged 55 or older take part in social and recreational activities at its Elderly Persons Centre. The facility also has a residential training centre where adults with hearing impairment and one or more other disabilities learn independent living skills, a residential home for those who are mentally and/or physically impaired as well as hearing-impaired, and apartments for individuals or couples aged 60 or older.

The Canadian Cancer Society, 10 Alcorn Avenue, Suite 200, Toronto, Ontario M4V 3B1. Provincial and territorial head offices are located in Alberta/Northwest Territories (Calgary), British Columbia/Yukon (Vancouver), Manitoba (Winnipeg), New Brunswick (Saint John), Newfoundland and Labrador (St. John's), Nova Scotia (Halifax), Ontario (Toronto), Prince Edward Island (Charlottetown), Quebec (Montreal), and Saskatchewan (Regina). The society has many local branches. Through its scientific affiliate, the National Cancer Institute of Canada, it funds research into the causes, early diagnosis, and treatment of cancer. It lobbies on behalf of efforts to reduce the use of tobacco products. Its patient services program provides chances for people to live with their cancer as hopefully as possible; volunteers, many of whom have had cancer, meet with patients and their families to talk about the illness and to offer support. It also promotes group meetings as well as one-on-one encounters. In addition, the program disseminates educational materials about the disease and such matters as dressings, medications, and prostheses. The society also supports lodges that provide accommodation for patients who must travel away from home to receive treatment.

The Canadian Council of the Blind, 396 Cooper Street, Suite 405, Ottawa, Ontario K2P 2H7. Provincial and territorial head offices are located in Alberta (Calgary), British Columbia/Yukon (Vancouver), Manitoba (Brandon), New Brunswick (Bathurst), Newfoundland and Labrador (St. John's), Nova Scotia/Prince Edward Island (Amherst, Nova Scotia), Ontario (Kitchener), Quebec (Montreal), and Saskatchewan (Regina). The council operates many local clubs that meet monthly for social and recreational activities. They disseminate information and offer support to those recently rendered sight-impaired. The council also raises funds to help the blind in underdeveloped regions of the world. It joins with the Canadian National Institute for the Blind to organize special events, demonstrations, speakers, and other activities during White Cane Week, held annually in early February to raise public awareness of the capabilities and needs of the visually impaired. It also lobbies for change with both government and service agencies for the blind.

The Canadian Diabetes Association, 78 Bond Street, Toronto, Ontario M5B 2J8. Provincial head offices are located in Alberta (Edmonton), British Columbia (Vancouver), Manitoba (Winnipeg), New Brunswick (Fredericton), Newfoundland (St. John's), Nova Scotia (Halifax), Ontario (Toronto), Prince Edward Island (Charlottetown), Quebec (Montreal), and Saskatchewan (Saskatoon). The association has many local branches. It provides ongoing information on diabetes to the more than 50,000 health care professionals who are members, and is Canada's second-largest (after government) supporter of research into the causes and treatment of diabetes. As the primary source of information and guidance for people with diabetes and their caregivers, it publishes a quarterly magazine, *Diabetes Dialogue*, and other educational reading materials and videos (see Chapter 13), and provincial and branch newsletters. It operates community centres that sell diabetes-related supplies. As well, it runs an ongoing advocacy program to ensure that people with diabetes are not discriminated against.

The Canadian Hearing Society, 271 Spadina Road, Toronto, Ontario M5R 2V3. The society has branches in the following Ontario centres: Barrie, Belleville, Brantford, Cambridge, Chatham, Fort Frances, Hamilton, Kenora, Kingston, London, North Bay, Ottawa, Peel, Peterborough, St. Catharines, Sarnia, Sault Ste. Marie, Sudbury, Thunder Bay, Toronto, Waterloo, and Windsor. It provides hearing tests, and hearing-aid evaluation, repair, and loan services. It sells a wide range of assistive aids and devices for those with hearing loss. It also runs a community outreach program to help elderly people who have hearing loss and offers training in lipreading and sign language. It disseminates information on hearing loss via pamphlets, books, films, videos, and a quarterly magazine, *Vibrations* (see Chapter 13). Its program for the elderly includes individual and group counselling on hearing loss and strategies for coping, assessments and referrals, and presentations and displays on aging and hearing loss.

The Canadian Hemochromatosis Society, Box 94303, Richmond, British Columbia V6Y 2A6. Branch offices exist in several centres, but since, at the time of writing, they are staffed entirely by volunteers, inquiries should be made of the head office. Hemochromatosis, the most common genetic disorder afflicting Canadians, is a crippling and potentially fatal disease caused by iron overload. It is treatable if diagnosed early, but many physicians are not knowledgeable about it. Symptoms include a sudden onset of diabetes, "bronzing" of the skin, arthritis, cirrhosis and other liver diseases, and chronic fatigue. The society produces literature on the disease for both lay people and professionals. It operates a referral service for those wishing to find a knowledgeable physician, and helps those who may have the disorder to find access to the correct testing and screening procedures.

The Canadian Liver Foundation, 1320 Yonge Street, Suite 301, Toronto, Ontario M4T 1X2. The foundation has chapters in Alberta (Calgary and Edmonton), British Columbia (Nanaimo, Vancouver, and Victoria), Manitoba (Winnipeg), New Brunswick (Fredericton, Moncton, and Saint John), Newfoundland (St. John's), Nova Scotia (Halifax), Ontario (Cornwall, Deep River, Hamilton-Wentworth, Kitchener-Waterloo, London, Mississauga, Niagara Region, Ottawa-Carleton, Sarnia-Lambton, Sudbury, Thunder Bay, and Toronto), Quebec (Montreal), and Saskatchewan (Regina and Saskatoon). The foundation helps set up support groups for people with liver diseases and their caregivers. It offers educational programs for the general public, people with liver disease, and the medical profession. It publishes a newsletter, *Communiqué* (see Chapter 13). It also funds research into liver diseases and liver function.

The Canadian Lung Association, 1900 City Park Drive, Suite 508, Blair Business Park, Gloucester, Ontario K1J 1A3. Provincial associations are located in Alberta (Edmonton), British Columbia (Vancouver), Manitoba (Winnipeg), New Brunswick (Fredericton), Newfoundland (St. John's), Nova Scotia (Halifax), Ontario (Toronto), Prince Edward Island (Charlottetown), Quebec (Montreal), Saskatchewan (Saskatoon), and Yukon (Whitehorse). The association has many local branches. It raises funds for medical research into respiratory problems. Through various leaflets and booklets, it disseminates information about diseases and conditions of the lungs, and ways in which to promote respiratory health. It acts as an advocate for those with lung problems, for instance, by promoting Better Breathing Month, during which motorists are asked to cycle, walk, or take public transit instead of driving. It also runs stop-smoking clinics and seminars on lung conditions and respiratory health.

The Canadian Mental Health Association, 2160 Yonge Street, Toronto, Ontario M4S 2Z3. Provincial and territorial branches are located in Alberta (Edmonton), British Columbia (Vancouver), Manitoba (Winnipeg), New Brunswick (Fredericton), Newfoundland (St. John's), Northwest Territories (Yellowknife), Nova Scotia (Halifax), Ontario (Toronto), Prince Edward Island (Charlottetown), Quebec (Montreal), Saskatchewan (Regina), and Yukon (Whitehorse). The association has many local branches. It sets up grass roots programs right across Canada to make sure that those with mental health problems can find the help they need to cope, then to regain confidence and return to normal. Programs include retirement counselling, crisis intervention, and friendly "helping hands" projects offering family-style support to patients who are separated from their own families. The association acts as an advocate on behalf of those with mental health problems at all three levels of government. It sponsors research into the causes of breakdown and despair and of emotional illness, and into patterns of living that will aid in recovery. As part of its ongoing programs of education, it also publishes informational leaflets and a newsletter (see Chapter 13).

The Canadian National Institute for the Blind, 1931 Bayview Avenue, Toronto, Ontario M4G 4C8. Division offices are located in Alberta-Northwest Territories (Edmonton), British Columbia-Yukon (Vancouver), Manitoba (Winnipeg), New Brunswick (Fredericton), Newfoundland and Labrador (St. John's), Nova Scotia-Prince Edward Island (Halifax), Ontario (Toronto), Quebec (Montreal), and Saskatchewan (Regina). The institute works to improve the condition of those with vision problems, using a team approach whereby staff, volunteers, and clients work together toward a set of common goals. The aim is to help those who are partially or wholly visually impaired to achieve the kind of life they want, in the home and in the community. Its technicians provide guidance about and demonstrations of a variety of assistive aids and devices. As well as operating a national mail-order lending service, its library lends books and magazines in braille and audio-cassette format. The library also provides talking-book cassette players and responds to requests to transcribe (from print to braille or audio-cassette format) vocational, educational, and professional materials. CNIB rehabilitation teachers go into clients' homes to demonstrate techniques and devices that will help clients function as best as possible when maintaining personal hygiene, preparing food, keeping house, handling money, and performing other daily routines. The CNIB sells more than 400 products to help those with vision impairment, among them talking watches, needle threaders, adapted games, and braille and large-print calendars. It operates the Lake Joseph Centre in central Ontario, where clients and their families can enjoy many activities, among them boating, canoeing, crafts, fitness programs, sailing, swimming, and waterskiing.

Communicaid for Hearing Impaired Persons, (CHIP) 3500 Decarie Boulevard, Montreal, Quebec H4A 3J5. CHIP runs classes and workshops on hearing-related topics, such as communication strategies, signing, speechreading, assertiveness training, emotional adjustment to hearing loss, and hearing and other assistive aids. Its members enjoy social activities, such as watching captioned feature films. CHIP also provides hearing-impaired people with information on government financial support and services, educates the general public on the potentials and problems of hearing-impaired people, encourages rehabilitation centres and homes for the elderly to run workshops at which staff learn about the special needs of those with hearing impairment, and generally lobbies for better conditions for those with impaired hearing.

The Crohn's and Colitis Foundation of Canada, 21 St. Clair Avenue East, Suite 301, Toronto, Ontario M4T 1L9. Regional offices are: Western (Calgary), Central (Winnipeg), Ontario (Toronto), Quebec (Montreal), Maritime (Halifax), and Newfoundland/Labrador (Bishop's Falls). The foundation has many local chapters. It raises funds for medical research into the causes of and potential cures for inflammatory bowel diseases. It disseminates information about such diseases widely through leaflets, films, videos, and *The CCFC Journal* (published quarterly; see Chapter 13). Each chapter holds quarterly educational meetings for members who have these diseases, their caregivers and other family members, health care professionals, and the general public. The foundation also has an advocacy role, working with physicians and volunteers to make representations to government, the insurance industry, and other relevant organizations on such matters as high medication and nutrient costs, the availability of insurance for patients, and human and civil rights for patients.

Deaf and Hard of Hearing Services (DHHS), Southern Alberta Deaf Centre, 63 Cornell Road N.W., Calgary, Alberta T2L 0L4. DHHS works with hearing-impaired people, providing interpreters, demonstrating effective assistive aids, assisting self-help groups to become established, training speechreading tutors, and running speechreading classes. It also disseminates information about deafness and impaired hearing, and functions as an advocacy group.

Epilepsy Canada, 1470 Peel Street, Suite 745, Montreal, Quebec H3A 1T1. Provincial offices are located in Alberta (Calgary), British Columbia (New Westminster), Manitoba (Winnipeg), New Brunswick (Saint John), Newfoundland and Labrador (St. John's), Nova Scotia (Halifax), Ontario (Willowdale), Prince Edward Island (Charlottetown), Quebec (Montreal), and Saskatchewan (Regina). The association has many local branches and support groups. It gives professional counselling to individuals with epilepsy, to caregivers and other family members, and to groups. It runs support groups and holds seminars on the psychosocial issues of epilepsy. It provides information on epilepsy to the public at large in various ways, among them printed materials and educational events and exhibits.

Hard of Hearing and Oral Deaf Services, c/o The Society for Manitobans with Disabilities Inc., 825 Sherbrook Street, Winnipeg, Manitoba R3A 1M5. Toll-free number for all of Manitoba, 1-800-282-8041. Branches are located in Brandon, Steinbach, Thompson, and Winnipeg. This organization runs classes on how to cope with hearing impairment, and also holds family meetings at which family members learn to understand the problems of hearing-impaired people and ways to help them.

The Heart and Stroke Foundation of Canada, 160 George Street, Suite 200, Ottawa, Ontario K1N 9M2. Provincial foundations are located in Alberta (Calgary), British Columbia and Yukon (Vancouver), Manitoba (Winnipeg), New Brunswick (Saint John), Newfoundland (St. John's), Nova Scotia (Halifax), Ontario (Toronto), Prince Edward Island (Charlottetown), Quebec (Montreal), and Saskatchewan (Saskatoon). The foundation has many regional offices. It raises funds for heart and stroke research, and educates the general public on the prevention, intervention, and rehabilitation aspects of heart disease and stroke. As well as printed materials, educational aspects include the administration of cardiopulmonary resuscitation courses, and a course that shows how to recognize the signs of a heart attack and how to get help fast. The foundation also runs an eight-week education program of information and support for cardiac patients and their partners or caregivers.

The Island Deaf and Hard of Hearing Centre (IDHHC), #211-55 Victoria Road, Nanaimo, British Columbia V9R 5N9, and #120-812 Wharf Street, Victoria, British Columbia V8W 1T3. IDHHC provides services and facilities for hearing-impaired people the length and breadth of Vancouver Island. It provides them with interpreting services, and its audiologist counsels those with hearing impairment and their families on how to cope with hearing loss, communication difficulties, and the choices of hearing aids, as well as demonstrating listening devices and holding communication strategy classes. A rehabilitation counsellor assesses individuals' skills and abilities, develops training plans to match individuals' goals, helps individuals to find funds for training, and provides generally supportive counselling. A vocational counsellor helps clients to get jobs, provides interpreters for job interviews, and arranges job coaching, if needed.

The Kidney Foundation of Canada, 5160 Decarie Boulevard, Suite 780, Montreal, Quebec H3X 2H9. Branch and chapter offices are located in British Columbia (Vancouver), Calgary and southern Alberta (Calgary), central Alberta (Red Deer), central Ontario (Don Mills), eastern Ontario (Ottawa), Edmonton and northern Alberta (Edmonton), greater Ontario (Toronto), Lethbridge (Lethbridge), Manitoba (Winnipeg), New Brunswick (Fredericton), Newfoundland (St. John's), Nova Scotia (Halifax), Prince Edward Island (Charlottetown), Quebec (Montreal), and Saskatchewan (Saskatoon). The foundation has many local branches. It provides patients and their caregivers, family members, and friends with emotional, educational, and material support. Educational tools include a manual which covers many topics, among them nutrition, blood chemistry, medications, and lifestyles, and a number of brochures on various kidney diseases. Dialysis vacations organized at places across Canada give patients an opportunity to enjoy a holiday while still receiving vital treatment. The foundation makes interest-free loans to patients who travel, to cover the cost of dialysis outside the country; patients repay the loans when they are reimbursed by their provincial health care plans. It operates peer support programs, providing ongoing help to patients, their families, and friends who are trying to cope with the effects of kidney disease. It is an advocate for patients with kidney disease. It provides medic alert bracelets to patients, runs audiovisual and print lending libraries, and publishes local newsletters. It also organizes hypertension testing clinics.

(There is a strong relationship between hypertension, or high blood pressure, and kidney disease.) It also publishes two newsletters (see Chapter 13). Most branches hold various social events.

The Newfoundland Coordinating Council on Deafness (NCCD), Ashley Building, Peet Street, P.O. Box 9125, St. John's, Newfoundland A1A 2X3. NCCD plays an advocacy role on behalf of hearing-impaired people. Trained staff perform vocational evaluations to establish recommendations for suitable vocational training. Employment counsellors help those having difficulty in the labour market. Interpreters work in many areas, among them employment interviews, health and dental care, social services, banking and other financial transactions, and legal matters.

The Newfoundland Hearing Association, P.O. Box 5203, St. John's, Newfoundland A1C 5V5. The association's objective is to improve the quality of life for all hearing-impaired people. It runs programs and services in both Newfoundland and Labrador. Among them is Hearing Helpers, a visiting service for elderly people, which operates in the following communities and surrounding areas: Bonavista, Carbonear, Clarenville, Corner Brook, Gander, Grand Falls, Lewisporte, Marystown, Placentia, St. John's, and Springdale. Hearing

Helpers are volunteer elders who discuss hearing loss, related problems, and possible solutions with those being visited. They impart effective communication strategies, demonstrate various assistive aids and show how to care for those chosen, and generally assist those with hearing impairment to maintain their independence. The association also runs an assistive-device loan program and functions as an advocate for those who are hard of hearing, arguing for such improvements as the availability of hearing-aid services and assistive devices in public buildings.

The Osteoporosis Society of Canada, P.O. Box 280, Station Q, Toronto, Ontario M4T 2M1. Several local branches are staffed by volunteers, so if you want information about the society, please contact the head office at the address given above. The society functions as a resource for people with osteoporosis, health care professionals, and the media. Many of its leaflets and booklets are available free of charge. It charges a small fee for videos on nutrition, exercise, and coping with osteoporosis. A semi-annual bulletin goes out to physicians and contains the latest information on diagnosis, therapeutic choices, and methods of prevention. The society considers prevention to be key: local volunteers help set up self-help and support groups for members of the public who want to learn from the experiences of others. It also raises funds for research into the disease, and helps those with osteoporosis and their caregivers set up support groups.

The Parkinson Foundation of Canada, 55 Bloor Street West, Suite 230, Toronto, Ontario M4W 1A5. Chapters and support groups are located across Canada; for information about either, use the foundation's toll-free number, 1-800-565-3000. The foundation raises funds to support research into the cause, treatment, and—it is to be hoped—ultimately a cure for Parkinson's disease. It publishes, and distributes to individuals and organizations, literature on the disease. It operates a wide range of services to help those with Parkinson's disease, their caregivers, and their families. It organizes training sessions and workshops for patients, caregivers, and health care providers. It contributes to a heightened awareness of the disease through local chapters and communities and a national campaign, and by fulfilling speaking engagements at hospitals, medical and health centres, nursing homes, and service clubs.

The Provincial Audiology Clinic, 65 McGill Avenue, Charlottetown, Prince Edward Island C1A 2K1. Services at the clinic include hearing tests and counselling as to appropriate hearing aids to use. Clients also can receive some general counsel on how to cope with hearing loss.

Saint John Deaf and Hard of Hearing Services Inc. (SJDHHS), 680 Ready Street, Saint John, New Brunswick E2M 3S5. SJDHHS's goal is to help those with hearing impairment to live independent and productive lives, and to ensure they have full access to the services and opportunities enjoyed by the hearing population. It runs workshops, information booths, and training programs to help bridge the communication gap between hearing and hearing-impaired people. A counsellor helps clients to acquire the necessary skills to obtain employment, among them how to fill out applications and interview techniques. The organization provides interpreters to work in a variety of settings, including legal, medical, and community. It disseminates information as requested on such matters as sign language, technical devices, lipreading, and self-help strategies. It also sells a variety of technical assistive devices.

Saskatchewan Deaf and Hard of Hearing Services Inc. (SDHHS), 2341 Broad Street, Regina, Saskatchewan S4P 1Y9, and 115 2nd Avenue North, Suite 301, Saskatoon, Saskatchewan S7K 2B1. SDHHS social workers counsel hearing-impaired people who have problems in such areas as health and medical issues, legal matters, substance abuse, depression, and housing. Its vocational rehabilitation counsellors help clients with job placement and general employment counselling. SDHHS also runs an interpretation service, and disseminates information on hearing loss in general and on assistive devices.

The Simon Foundation of Canada, P.O. Box 264, Station E, Toronto, Ontario M6H 4E2. Toll-free number: 1-800-265-9575. The foundation disseminates information about urinary incontinence (which anywhere from 40 to 60 per cent of the Canadian population will experience at some time). It gives counsel to those who have this problem. At the time of writing, it was starting to organize self-help groups across the country.

The Society for Manitobans with Disabilities, 825 Sherbrook Street, Winnipeg, Manitoba R3A 1M5. Regional offices are located in Brandon, Dauphin, Thompson, and Steinbach. The society holds speechreading classes for those with hearing impairment, and also assists clients with rehabilitation and vocational counselling. In general, it helps those with hearing impairment to develop the skills they need to remain independent within the community.

The Society of Deaf and Hard of Hearing Nova Scotians, Roy Building, 1657 Barrington Street, Suite 101, Halifax, Nova Scotia B3J 2A1. The society provides interpreters for help in a variety of situations. A program called Silent Reach helps those with hearing impairments living in Metro Halifax to solve job-related problems or to find employment. A program called Project Access advises people with hearing impairment where they can get assistance to solve problems.

The United Ostomy Association of Canada Inc., 5 Hamilton Avenue, Hamilton, Ontario L8V 2S3. The association has many local chapters, but no regional or provincial offices. It helps those who have had ostomy surgery (surgery in which internal or external pouches are fitted to patients who, for whatever reason, cannot excrete waste matter normally). Members meet regularly, often to hear guest speakers, and to exchange information and experiences with their ostomies. The association disseminates information about ostomies in the form of leaflets, pamphlets, and books, all suitable material for the lay reader.

The Western Institute for the Deaf and Hard of Hearing, 2125 West 7th Avenue, Vancouver, British Columbia V6K 1X9. The institute has a wide range of services and programs to help those with hearing impairment. Its counselling services are numerous and include psychological and psychiatric assessment; therapy for individuals, couples, and families; training in life, social, and personal skills; restoration counselling; and general consultation. Its audiology services include hearing tests, hearing-aid evaluations, and hearing-aid trials under supervision. (The institute also sells and services hearing aids and technical assistive devices of various types.) Its interpreter services are used in a variety of situations, among them medical, mental health, and legal. It also has a wide range of employment services.

CHAPTER FIVE

HELP FOR TROUBLED MINDS

AS WE AGE, WE SHALL ALL EXPERIENCE A SERIES OF losses. Parents first, perhaps, and other elderly relatives and friends. Upon retirement, the career—often a grave loss for professionals and people in management who identify themselves by their positions. Gone too is the high income the career provided. Then robust health, siblings, a spouse.

Given all these potential losses, no one should be surprised to learn that many elderly people suffer from depression, which is probably the most common psychological problem in later life.

Substance dependency and abuse constitute another common problem. Elderly people may turn to alcohol to blur the pain of losses and lighten the burden of depression. As well, many become addicted to medications—prescribed ones, such as tranquillizers, or over-the-counter ones, such as sleeping pills. The use of both these classes of drugs increases with age. (Ironically, some medications can cause depression. The result is a vicious circle, with an unfortunate elder trapped inside it.)

Anxieties that were mild in early life can turn into disabling phobias and fears in later life. People who never had them before may start having panic attacks.

Some elderly people who experience considerable memory loss may fear they are developing Alzheimer's or some other form of dementia. And indeed, some *will* develop dementia of one kind or another.

Clearly, there are plenty of reasons for elderly people to have troubled minds. Fortunately, there are also plenty of places they or their caregivers can turn to in order to receive help.

KNOCKING ON THE FIRST DOOR

In many cases, the appropriate first door to knock on is that of the elder's family physician. Unless you really have no choice, do not make an appointment to see her or him by yourself; rather, see the physician together. Discuss what appear to be problem areas, and seek advice. If a psychiatrist or a psychotherapist should be consulted, the physician may be able to recommend one—and will almost certainly have to write a letter of referral to the specialist.

A public health nurse, reached via the local board of health or health care services department (see Chapter 1), can perform the same function as a family physician.

ASSESSMENT SERVICES

Assessment services for elders are available in some locations. Staff interview elders, then refer them on to appropriate treatment centres. For instance, a client who may be drinking heavily but may also be profoundly depressed or have some other psychiatric problem will be referred on to a place where both psychiatric and substance-abuse counselling are available. Toronto has the Metro Addiction Assessment Referral Service. Similar services exist in about 35 other centres across Ontario; to find them, look in the telephone directory, where they will usually be listed as "Addiction Assessment Referral Service," probably preceded by the name of the city, town, or region. Halifax has an assessment service, operated by the Drug Dependency Services Division of the provincial Department of Health. Assessments are made at the numerous outpatient departments of the Health Promotion and Disease Prevention Division of the New Brunswick Department of Health and Community Services; at the Alcoholism Treatment Centre in Charlottetown, Prince Edward Island; and at 11 community health services branches of the Saskatchewan Alcohol and Drug Abuse Commission.

SELF-HELP GROUPS

Self-help is one of the most valuable forms of aid for anyone, and especially for older people. Those involved in self-help groups remain in charge of their own lives and achieve a sense of well-being through sharing thoughts and experiences, through helping and being helped simultaneously. For an older person, this form of help is far more acceptable than being placed in a subordinate position to a helper who is likely to be much younger.

Self-help groups for elders are becoming numerous: there are about 80 in Metro Toronto alone. They address many issues, among them depression, phobias, isolation, bereavement, and other problems that cause troubled minds.

How do you find an appropriate self-help group in your area? Here is a list of clearinghouses or self-help resource centres, furnished by Self-Help Canada, the national organization. Note that some of these clearinghouses and centres, while in existence at time of writing, are dependent on funding and may close down at any time. If this is the case in your area, and/or if you would like to find out whether a new centre has recently opened locally, write to Self-Help Canada at P.O. Box 64094, 1620 Scott Street, Ottawa, Ontario K1Y 4V1.

Alberta

Castle Downs Centre, 15277 113A Street, Suite 124, Edmonton, Alta. T5X 3N5

Family Life Education Council of Calgary, 233 12th Avenue SW, Calgary, Alta. T2R 0G9

British Columbia

The Self-Help Resource Association of British Columbia, 175 West Broadway, Vancouver, B.C. V5Y 1P4

Manitoba

Manitoba Clearinghouse Concerning Disabilities Inc., 825 Sherbrook Street, Winnipeg, Man. R3A 1M5

New Brunswick

Human Development Council, Box 6125, Station A, Saint John, N.B. E2L 4R6

Nova Scotia

Self-Help Connection, Canadian Mental Health Association, Nova Scotia Division, 63 King Street, Dartmouth, N.S. B2Y 2R7

Ontario

Canadian Mental Health Association, York Region, 200 Davis Drive, Newmarket, Ont. L3Y 2N4

Office of the Vice-Rector, Laurentian University, 935 Ramsay Lake Road, Sudbury, Ont. P3E 1C5

Self-Help Clearinghouse, Canadian Mental Health Association, Waterloo Region, 607 King Street West, Kitchener, Ont. N2G 1T6

Self-Help Clearinghouse of Metro Toronto, 40 Orchard View Boulevard, Suite 219, Toronto, Ont. M4R 1B9

Self-Help Network, 592 Adelaide Street, Woodstock, Ont. N4S 4B9

The Olde Forge Community Resource Centre, 2730 Carling Avenue, Ottawa, Ont. K2B 7J1

Prince Edward Island

Canadian Mental Health Association, P.O. Box 785, Charlottetown, P.E.I. C1A 7L9

Quebec

CAP Santé Outaouais, 672 St-Joseph Boulevard, Hull, Que. J8Y 4A8

Centre d'Action bénévol du Québec, 615 Pierre Bertrand Boulevard, Quebec City, Que. G1M 1M6

Centre du Référence du Grand Montréal, 881 Maisonneuve Boulevard E., Montreal, Que. H2L 1Y8

West Island Community Resource Centre, 81 Summerhill, Pointe Claire, Que. H9R 2L4

COPING WITH ANXIETY DISORDERS

Anxiety disorders now constitute this country's leading mental illness, ahead of both depression and substance abuse. So far, self-help groups for those with this problem are thin on the ground, but at least a start has been made, and almost certainly more groups will come into being. One of the first Canadian organizations—if not *the* first—was the Free From Fear Foundation in Pickering, Ontario. As well, there is the Agoraphobic Foundation of Canada in Laval, Quebec; Secure Program in Burnaby, British Columbia; and the Freedom From Fear Foundation in Toronto.

If you want to find out whether a new group has come into being in your area since this book was written, write to the Free From Fear Foundation at 1400 Bayly Street, Unit 15A, Pickering, Ontario L1W 3R2. Or contact your local Canadian Mental Health Association office or a self-help clearinghouse.

THE ANONYMOUS SELF-HELP GROUPS

Almost certainly you will have heard of Alcoholics Anonymous (AA), the organization with local groups in thousands of communities right around the world, at whose meetings alcoholics and recovering alcoholics talk about their experiences and in so doing help themselves and others in the group resolve to be sober. Meetings are open (people who are not AA members may attend) or closed (for AA members only). There are no fees; most groups "pass the hat" to raise funds to defray meeting costs—and, typically, to make a contribution to the fellowship's national and international services.

Less well known is Narcotics Anonymous (NA). NA groups exist in most large centres in Canada. The organization is for those who feel they have become addicted to any mood-altering substance, including alcohol. It functions in the same way as AA, with open and closed meetings, and voluntary contributions.

To find a local group of either AA or NA, look in your telephone directory.

Also less well known than AA is Emotions Anonymous (EA). EA exists to help those who suffer from depression, fear, anxiety, anger, or any other debilitating emotion. It functions in much the same way as AA.

You will not find EA groups listed in the telephone directory. Instead, call your nearest self-help clearinghouse (see above, pages 62-64) and ask if there is an EA group in your community and, if so, how you and/or your elder can contact it.

RECOVERY INC.

This organization exists to help those suffering from depression, fear, or anxiety. Unlike AA and NA meetings, Recovery meetings are structured; discussion leaders are generally trained. Anyone can join a group; referrals are not necessary. There are no membership fees, but people usually contribute a small amount to defray meeting costs. Groups exist in Alberta, British Columbia, New Brunswick, Newfoundland, Ontario, Prince Edward Island, Quebec, and Saskatchewan.

To find out if there is a group in your area and, if so, how to contact it, consult with the self-help clearinghouse nearest you.

BY OURSELVES

By Ourselves is a self-help club in Regina for people with psychiatric problems. It operates a drop-in centre for attendees, where lunch is served daily. It is also a food-bank distributor and an advocate for the rights of those with psychiatric problems. For more information, contact By Ourselves at 2054 Broad Street, Regina, Saskatchewan S4P 1Y3.

TELEPHONE HELP

Tel-Aide in Montreal helps people who are depressed, lonely, or troubled, who are perhaps without hope and near the end of their tether. Such people phone in and talk to sympathetic and supportive listeners. Help is thus immediate, and Tel-Aide guarantees anonymity and confidentiality. The service is an around-the-clock one, and may be accessed by anyone living in Greater Montreal or Laval, or on the South Shore.

For more information, write to Tel-Aide at P.O. Box 205, Station H, Montreal, Quebec H3G 2K5.

The Shalom Line, operated by the Jewish Community Listening Service, also offers support via the telephone to those who live in Montreal. It is used by, among others, people experiencing depression, loneliness, suicidal thoughts, and problems with alcohol or drugs. It too guarantees anonymity and confidentiality. The service operates from 4:30 p.m. to 10:30 p.m. Mondays through Thursdays and from 10:30 a.m. to 4:30 p.m. on Sundays.

For more information, contact the Jewish Community Listening Service at 5150 Côte Ste. Catherine, Montreal, Quebec H1V 2A5.

COPE

COPE is a program in the Durham region of Ontario whose goal is to help adults with emotional or mental problems to remain in the community by teaming them up on a one-on-one basis with volunteers trained in communication and life skills. In some areas, COPE also organizes social, recreational, and/or support groups. The interactions between clients and volunteer counsellors are closely supervised by trained professionals. When the person being helped is elderly, a referral is often made by the family physician. Those using COPE's services pay nothing; the program is funded by the Ontario Ministry of Health.

For more information, contact COPE administrators at one of the following Durham regional Community Care offices:

Ajax/Pickering—122 Hunt Street, Ajax, Ont. L1S 1P5
Brock—24 Cameron Street West, Cannington, Ont. L0E 1E0
Newcastle—98 King Street West, Bowmanville, Ont. L1C 1R4
Oshawa—45 Bloor Street East, Oshawa, Ont. L1H 3L9
Scugog—175 North Street, Port Perry, Ont. L9L 1B7
Uxbridge—56 Brock Street West, Box 1706, Uxbridge, Ont. L0C 1K0
Whitby—209 Dundas Street East, Suite 3, Whitby, Ont. L1N 7H8

SOCIAL DAY AT THE "Y"

Social Day at the "Y" is a daytime program for elderly people in Montreal who are depressed, isolated, and/or needing socialization. They meet once a week, from mid-morning to mid-afternoon, for activities, including discussion groups, day trips, physical exercises, and self-help groups.

For more information, contact Jewish Support Services for the Elderly at 5500 Westbury Avenue, Montreal, Quebec H3W 3G2.

BEREAVEMENT PROGRAM

For those living in or near St. John's, Newfoundland, the Seniors Resource Centre runs a bereavement program. Bereaved people meet in small groups of no more than ten, on eight occasions. Groups are led by a professional who is experienced in grief counselling, and other people from the community with expertise come in to address specific concerns. Transportation is provided free of charge if necessary. Confidentiality is guaranteed.

For more information, contact the Seniors Resource Centre at 120 Torbay Road, Suite 104, St. John's, Newfoundland A1A 2G8.

NEW BEGINNINGS

The Beginning Experience helps widowed, divorced, and

separated people in Prince Edward Island make a new start in life through an intense, positive experience of hope. A weekend program held three times a year—in spring, fall, and midwinter—it was originally designed by and for Roman Catholics, but is open to men and women of all faiths.

For more information, contact Mrs. Jean Blanchard, 138 Upper Prince Street, Charlottetown, Prince Edward Island C1A 4S7.

SUBSTANCE-ABUSE SERVICES AND FACILITIES

Nearly one in ten Canadians over 60 years of age has a substance-abuse problem. Fortunately, both residential and outpatient treatment centres abound.

Probably the best-known of the organizations that provide treatment for substance abusers and also fund and carry out research and advocacy programs is the Addiction Research Foundation in Toronto. It is one of the larger and older of such organizations and has treated many people with substance-abuse problems, including people from outside Toronto and southern Ontario.

Provincial and territorial government departments run detoxification and rehabilitation programs, on both an outpatient and a residential basis, and typically do not require a referral from a physician or other health care professional. They also disseminate information on substance abuse. Here's a list of whom to contact for information and literature.

Alberta

Alberta Alcohol and Drug Abuse Commission, 10909 Jasper Avenue, 7th Floor, Edmonton, Alta. T5J 3M9

British Columbia

Alcohol and Drug Programs, Ministry of Labour and Consumer Affairs, 1019 Wharf Street, 6th Floor, Victoria, B.C. V8V 1X4

Also B.C. Prevention Resource Centre, 96 East Broadway, Suite 108, Vancouver, B.C. V5T 1V6

Manitoba

Alcoholism Foundation of Manitoba, 1031 Portage Avenue, 3rd Floor, Winnipeg, Man. R3G 0R8

New Brunswick

Health Promotion and Disease Prevention, Department of Health and Community Services, P.O. Box 5100, 520 King Street, Carleton Place, Fredericton, N.B. E3B 5G8

Newfoundland

Drug Dependency Services, Department of Health, 1st Floor, West Block, Confederation Building, P.O. Box 8700, St. John's, Nfld. A1B 4J6

Also Humberwood Drug Dependency Service, 169 West Valley Road, Corner Brook, Nfld. A2H 2Y3

Northwest Territories

Alcohol, Drugs and Community Mental Health Programs, 6th Floor, Precambrian Building, 52nd Street, P.O. Box 1320, Yellowknife, NWT X1A 2L9

Nova Scotia

Drug Dependency Services, 6th Floor, Lord Nelson Building, 5675 Spring Garden Road, Halifax, N.S. B3J 1H1

Ontario

Addiction Research Foundation, 33 Russell Street, Toronto, Ont. M5S 2S1

Prince Edward Island

Alcohol & Drug Problems Institute, Beach Grove Road, Charlottetown, P.E.I. C1A 7K7

Also Prince County Addiction Services, 216 Schurman Avenue, Summerside, P.E.I. C1N 4W6; *and* Kings County Addiction Services, Breakwater Street, P.O. Box 100, Souris, P.E.I. C0A 2B0

Quebec

Programs for Substance Abusers, Ministry of Health and Social Services, 1005 Ste-Foy, Quebec City, Que. G1S 4N4

Saskatchewan

Saskatchewan Alcohol and Drug Abuse Commission, 1942 Hamilton Street, Regina, Sask. S4P 3V7

Yukon

Alcohol and Drug Services, Yukon Department of Health and Human Resources, P.O. Box 2703, 6118 6th Avenue, Whitehorse, Yukon Y1A 2C6

Of private organizations running both residential and outreach programs for substance abusers, probably the best known is the Donwood Institute in Toronto. Donwood provides treatment for those abusing alcohol or drugs (including prescribed medications). In the residential program, clients live at the institute for 28 days, then come in once a week in the evening for nine weeks. In the outpatient program, clients come in daily, Mondays through Fridays, from 8:00 a.m. to 4:00 p.m. for 16 days, then once a week in the evening for nine weeks. There is also an evening outpatient program, in which clients come in two evenings a week for three months. All programs are aimed at total abstinence; controlled drinking is not part of the institute's philosophy. For Ontario residents, all costs are covered by OHIP.

For more information, contact the institute at 175 Brentcliff Road, Toronto, Ontario M4G 3Z1

To find similar private facilities, contact the appropriate provincial organization listed on pages 71–2 to obtain a copy of its literature. In almost all cases, you will find private facilities included in the information provided.

SERVICES SPECIFICALLY FOR ADDICTED ELDERLY PEOPLE

More often than not, these are small, even one-person organizations, operating on a shoestring budget, and typically providing outreach services for elderly people with substance-abuse problems.

One such is Community Older Persons Alcohol Program (COPA) in Toronto. A COPA staffer will go into an elder's home and, unlike Alcoholics Anonymous which requires members to admit to their problem and abstain from alcohol, will make no such demands. Instead, she or he will try to find out what lies behind the substance abuse and solve *that* problem, hoping that, in so doing, she or he will also help the client drink more sparingly or quit entirely. Clients are also helped to find whatever help they need, be it housing, financial, or whatever, within the system. You can reach COPA at 27 Roncesvalles Avenue, Suite 407, Toronto, Ontario M6R 2K4.

The following organizations and individuals also have programs and services geared specifically to older clients:

- Addiction Services Inc. (Hastings and Prince Edward Counties), 158 George Street, Belleville, Ontario, K8N 3H3
- Shirley Congden, VISTA, Oak Bay Lodge, 2251 Cadboro Road, Victoria, British Columbia V8L 5H3
- Elders Health Program, 400 Tache Avenue, Suite 403, Winnipeg, Manitoba R2H 3C3
- Ellen Tabisz, Department of Social Work, St. Boniface Hospital, 409 Tache Avenue, Winnipeg, Manitoba R2H 2A6

- Lifestyle Enrichment for Senior Adults, Centretown Community Health Centre, 340 MacLaren Street, Ottawa, Ontario K2P 0M6
- Serenity Renewal for Families, 2810 Baycrest Drive, Ottawa, Ontario K1V 7P7
- Peggy Stauft, MSW, Calgary District Hospital Group, 1213 4th Street S.W., Calgary, Alberta T2R 0X7
- Matt Talbot Houses, 234 Carlton Street, Toronto, Ontario M5A 2L1

OTHER SUBSTANCE-ABUSE SERVICES AND INFORMATION

Women for Sobriety is an organization with groups in many provinces and territories, among them Alberta, British Columbia, Ontario, Saskatchewan, and Yukon. It is an alternative to Alcoholics Anonymous for those people who are not religious: AA members have to profess a belief in a higher being, although the nature of that being need not be specified.

For more information and to find out whether a group exists in your area, contact the North American head office at P.O. Box 618, Quakertown, Pennsylvania, U.S.A., 18951, or call its toll-free telephone number: 1-800-333-1606.

A parallel organization, Men for Sobriety, exists; at the time of writing, it appears that only one Canadian group is in operation, located in Kitchener, Ontario.

Like COPA (see above, page 74), DrinkWise is a program for those who want to cut back on their alcohol consumption but not necessarily abstain entirely. Clients are those who are developing an alcohol problem but are not yet alcoholics. They may be referred to the program by family physicians or others, or they may self-refer. Operated by parent organization Homewood Health Services, DrinkWise programs were available only in Ontario communities at the time of writing, but plans were to expand into other provinces.

For more information, contact Homewood Health Services, 150 Delhi Street, Guelph, Ontario N1E 6K9.

CHAPTER SIX

NEW AGE HEALTH AIDS

AMONG BOTH HEALTH CARE PROFESSIONALS AND lay people, a move toward a more holistic medical approach is clearly under way. Not all the new forms of treatment and therapy work for everyone, and they should not be used as replacements for more conventional forms of treatment. But in their efforts to retain good health in the later years, elderly people might well enjoy adding a new age health aid to the fitness programs and practices they already undertake.

PETS AS HEALTH PROMOTERS

Several studies have demonstrated that, without a doubt, pet-facilitated therapy, or PFT, is highly effective. One study showed that, of patients discharged from a hospital's coronary care unit, those who had pets were more likely to be alive one year later than were those who did not.

In another case, a variety of pets, among them birds, rabbits, and guinea pigs, was introduced into several of the wards at a hospital for the criminally insane. A review of the program showed that the convicted psychopaths on the wards into which pets had been introduced needed half as much medication as those on other wards. As well, they were far less violent and less likely to take their own lives.

Lowered blood pressure, better social interaction, and improved morale are other side-effects of pet ownership.

Many SPCA branches pair people up with pets. Contact your local branch. As well, several humane and other animal societies, among them the Toronto Humane Society, will match elderly people up with pets and provide neutering and inoculations at a reduced rate. Some veterinarians in private practice also offer elders discounted rates.

AROMAS AS ASSISTIVE AIDS

As numerous studies have shown, for reasons as yet unknown, certain fragrances have a relaxing effect on people, markedly reducing stress levels.

Massage therapists are increasingly using aromatic plant oils as they go about their work. Lavender is highly relaxing and is a good treatment for skin conditions, such as dryness and bed sores. Basil is a good tranquillizer, as is chamomile. Sage relieves muscular tension, while hyssop is believed to be good for the circulation. Lemon enhances the immune system, and bergamot, clove, and peppermint help the digestion.

As well as finding a massage therapist who uses aromatic oils, an elderly person might try breathing in certain beneficial fragrances. Peppermint and lily of the valley both appear to promote alertness, while spiced apple and vanilla lower stress levels and reduce anxiety.

Check your Yellow Pages under "Massage Therapists." Entries seldom indicate whether or not aromatherapy is offered, so you may have to make several calls before finding a therapist who practises it. Health food stores commonly sell aromatic oils.

HEALTH THROUGH HOMEOPATHY

Increasingly gaining in popularity, homeopathic medicine replaces or works alongside regular medications, using highly diluted doses of remedies from natural sources. Homeopathic remedies are prescribed under a principle known as "like curing like." In other words, a substance that will create certain undesirable symptoms in a well person will, when taken in minute doses, cure those same symptoms in a sick person.

Homeopathy is considered a part of mainstream medicine in many parts of the world. The reasons for its increased popularity in North America are twofold: unlike regular medications, homeopathic remedies have no side-effects, and they are often relatively inexpensive.

How do you determine whether a homeopathic practitioner is experienced and knowledgeable? One way is to opt to become a patient of a naturopath, a health professional trained in a number of natural healing methodologies, among them homeopathy. A certified naturopath will have the initials "N.D." after his or her name. To find naturopaths in your area, consult the Yellow Pages, or contact the Canadian Naturopaths Association at Box 4520, Station C, Calgary, Alberta T2T 5N3, or your provincial association of naturopathic practitioners: The Alberta Association of Naturopathic Practitioners, in Calgary; the Association of Naturopathic Physicians of British Columbia, in Vancouver; the Manitoba Association of Naturopathic Practitioners, in Winnipeg; the Maritime Association of Naturopathic Practitioners, in Berwick, Nova Scotia; the Ontario Naturopathic Association, in Toronto; the Quebec Association of Naturopathic Practitioners, in Knowlton; and the Saskatchewan Association of Naturopathic Physicians, in Saskatoon.

A COSMETIC BOOST FOR THOSE WITH CANCER

In 1992, the Canadian Cosmetic, Toiletry and Fragrance Association (CCTFA) launched a program called Look Good . . . Feel Better—and, indeed, patients who have had cancer and received radiation and/or chemotherapy treatments do seem to feel better when they use cosmetics to improve their appearance.

Among recommendations the CCTFA makes are:

- When you are going to be outdoors, use a sunscreen with SPF15 or more, since chemotherapy makes the skin more sun-sensitive.
- When applying cleansing products, do so gently, using an upward and outward motion to avoid damaging the delicate surface of the skin. Both chemotherapy and radiation can make the skin more susceptible to bruising.
- Use a cream or stick concealer under foundation to hide any blemishes or discolourations, or dark circles under the eyes.
- Use mascara to make thinning eyelashes look thicker.
- Use neutral eyeshadows that bring out the colour of the iris to improve the look of jaundiced eyes. Don't use blue, green, or purple eyeshadow.

To find out more about the CCFTA recommendations and/or to obtain a copy of an informative brochure entitled *Look Good . . . Feel Better*, write the association at 5090 Explorer Drive, Suite 510, Mississauga, Ontario L4W 4T9.

CHAPTER SEVEN

MAKING LIFE MORE COMFORTABLE

JUST AS SERVICES AND PROGRAMS FOR THE ELDERLY HAVE proliferated in recent years, so have the types of various assistive aids and devices, all designed to make life more comfortable and easier.

In general, devices have also become more attractive. For instance, in the past grab bars were always made of chromium-plated steel and had a cold, institutional look. Today, they are also made in gracefully sculpted shapes and out of strong white plastic. Similarly, motorized wheelchairs have become more streamlined and now resemble general-purpose scooters.

Here, first, is a rundown, in alphabetical order, of manufacturers and/or distributors of some of the more inventive and/or more frequently needed aids and devices, to give you an idea of what is available out there. Information on how to find retail outlets follows. Note that, unless a distributor is also clearly identified as a supplier (see, for example, the Canadian Institute for the Blind below), contact retail outlets first and manufacturers or distributors only if you can find no local retailer selling the item you want.

Finally, information is provided about organizations that will pay part or all of the cost of assistive devices, as well as about how to claim a rebate for money spent to improve or modify a home, perhaps so that someone in a wheelchair can move about freely.

MANUFACTURERS AND DISTRIBUTORS

Airway Surgical Appliances Ltd. of Nepean, Ontario, markets Embrace Air, an adjustable back support. The user turns a valve to adjust it to his or her personal comfort level. The cover is treated to render it immune to fungus and bacteria, and the device attaches to any chair and so can be used at home, in an automobile, or at the office.

For more information, if you live in western Canada or Newfoundland, dial toll-free 1-800-267-8098: if you live in central Canada or the Maritimes, dial 1-800-267-3476.

Bard Canada Inc. of Mississauga, Ontario, has developed the Contigen collagen implant to help those with urinary incontinence. The implant consists of highly purified collagen, a protein that is injected directly into the tissues surrounding the urethra, usually under a local anaesthetic on an outpatient basis. If you are giving care to someone with urinary incontinence, you or your care receiver should speak to the family physician about the possibility of a Contigen implant.

Bell Canada Inc. has many telephone devices to help people with disabilities. Among them are TEL-EASE, a telephone set with extra-large, easy-to-read push buttons, a ten-number memory, a ringer indicator light, and receiver volume control. The Walker 10 receiver amplifier, when attached to a regular telephone, increases the volume of incoming sound at the touch of a control knob. The Directel telephone is for people who cannot dial or hold a receiver. To place calls, the user simply blows into a small plastic tube; this connects him or her to an operator who will then dial the desired number.

These and other devices are available for purchase through Bell's Telecommunication Centre for Special Needs, Bell Trinity Square, Floor 1, North Tower, 483 Bay Street, Toronto, Ontario M5G 2E1. Other telephone companies in Canada have similar specialized equipment for subscribers with disabilities.

The Canadian Hearing Society has a catalogue describing more than 20 products it sells to help those with hearing disabilities. Watchman Masters converts sound to light, using existing house wiring; it can monitor a wide range of sounds, including a door bell, a telephone ring, or a baby's cry. The Silent Page consists of a wrist-worn vibrating receiver and a number of transmitters. The latter can be placed on a table or can be wall mounted and alerts the user to a range of sounds, such as a door bell or telephone ringing, or a smoke detector going off. The Bedshaker comprises a smoke detector, a receiver, and a vibrator; the user mounts the smoke detector in the desired position, plugs the receiver into a regular electrical outlet, and places the vibrator under the pillow or mattress. If the smoke detector goes off, a strong vibration will awaken the sleeping user.

You can obtain a copy of the catalogue by writing to the society's head office at 271 Spadina Road, Toronto, Ontario M5R 2V3, or by dialling its toll-free number, 1–800–465–4327, from anywhere in Canada.

The Canadian National Institute for the Blind has a wide range of assistive aids for those with impaired sight. They include talking and braille books and other literature, magnifiers with a light attachment, and binoculars and monoculars. Devices may be simple, such as a needle threader or a hand-held or stand magnifier, or highly complex, such as a machine that scans the printed word and repeats it back to the user, printers that produce text in braille, and closed-circuit TV readers that can magnify print up to 60 times.

To order, contact your local branch or write the national office at 1931 Bayview Avenue, Toronto, Ontario M4G 4C8.

Care Transportation International (C.T.I.) Ltd. custom-converts Chrysler vans for use by people with disabilities. The company lowers the floor and puts in a ramp so that someone in a wheelchair may ride as either the driver or a passenger. It removes the second-row bench seat and modifies the driver's and front passenger seats in such a way that a wheelchair can occupy either space. It will also lower just part of the floor, to accommodate a motor scooter perhaps.

For more information, contact the company at 5810 Côte de Liesse, Mt. Royal, Quebec H4T 1B1.

Diabetic Shoppes of Canada Limited has a full range of supplies for those with diabetes, including monitors and needles. Staff will show clients how to use the monitors if necessary. The company also fills mail orders.

For more information, write the company at 3539 Bathurst Street, Toronto, Ontario M6A 2C7.

Device Technologies Inc. of Scarborough, Ontario, has developed the Step Ease system which makes going up or down a staircase easier for those with hip or back problems or those who have reduced mobility in general. In essence, the system consists of a series of blocks forming ministeps. Each one is half the height of a regular riser. One is placed on the banister side of each tread. Since a user must lift or lower her or his foot only half the normal distance, limb movement is decreased. For additional safety, each block has a textured, rubberized, non-skid surface.

For more information, contact the company at 100 Dynamic Drive, Suite 202, Scarborough, Ontario M1V 5C4, or call the company's toll-free number, 1-800-563-7837, from anywhere in Canada.

Genus Medical Inc. manufactures the Flyer, a three-wheel scooter, and the Flyer 4, a four-wheel variation. Both are precision engineered, and both comprise five lightweight components that can be assembled and disassembled speedily, without tools, for easy portability.

For more information, contact the company at 441-A Applewood Crescent, Concord, Ontario L4K 4B4, or call its toll-free number, 1-800-567-9153 from anywhere in Canada.

Ginger Eisen's Bathrooms is the latest venture of 75-year-old Ginger Eisen who formerly owned and operated a luxury bathroom business called Ginger's. This time her theme is "bathrooms for the physically challenged." Among devices sold in the store: a cushioned bathtub with an acrylic skin and a foam core that is soft to the touch, a toilet with a shower spray and dryer that eliminates the need to use toilet paper, a wheel-in acrylic shower with a bench seat, sinks and toilet seats that raise and lower, and many types of tension poles and grab bars.

If you are interested in learning more, obtain a catalogue from the store at Hazelton Lanes, 87 Avenue Road, Toronto, Ontario M5R 3R9. You can also order items by mail.

Golden Boy Medical, like Care Transportation International (see above), custom-converts minivans for use by people with disabilities. It also converts both vans and cars by putting in special hand controls, relocating certain controls, and adding steering and driving devices that make operating the vehicle easier for those with some function impairment. As well, it has a line of home care products, among them stair and vertical lifts, portable and fixed ramps, bedroom and bathroom patient lifts, power door openers, wheelchairs, and scooters.

For more information, contact the company at 4912 93 Avenue, Edmonton, Alberta T6B 2L6, or, if you are calling from an Alberta exchange, dial the company's toll-free number: 1–800–282–3909.

Holl Meditronics of Bolton, Ontario, has several wheelchair attachments and devices. One is the Scala-mobil, a battery-powered accessory that permits a wheelchair to climb up to 300 steps on one battery charge. The device can be used on stone, carpet, and straight or circular steps, and can be operated by one person, regardless of the weight of the wheelchair user. Another is the Reck Motor-med, a machine that allows someone in a wheelchair to exercise arms and legs. For maximum value, the machine is operated manually, but those who have severely weakened limbs can derive benefit from using it electrically driven, to engage in passive exercise.

For more information and/or to obtain a catalogue, write the company at 4 Marconi Court, Bolton, Ontario L7E 1E7.

Invacare Corporation has the Avanti line of seating and positioning products used to accessorize wheelchairs. Among them are cushions of various kinds, backrests, and laptrays.

For more information, contact the company at 899 Cleveland Street, Elyria, Ohio, U.S.A., 44036, or call its toll-free number, 1-800-668-5324, from anywhere in Canada.

Kraftwerk is a one-man band, but the man, Riese Heemskerk, is inventive indeed. He has designed the Try Cycle and will custom-build the machine to clients' specifications. The Try Cycle is, in fact, a mountain bike with the front wheel removed and replaced with a frame and harness which can be adjusted to clamp onto the back of any wheelchair. While the caregiver riding the Try Cycle gets his or her exercise workout of the day, the person in the wheelchair is taken for a spin. The device is easily transportable since it folds into a car trunk. A power-assisted version is also available.

For more information, write to the company at 4259 William Street, Beamsville, Ontario L0R 1B0.

Medic Alert is an emergency medical information system. Members wear either a bracelet or a necklet identification tag. The Medic Alert symbol appears on the front of the tag; on the back, relevant medical information is engraved, as well as the member's identification number and an around-the-clock phone number anyone tending the member can use to obtain additional information. Members also carry a wallet card showing their medical records and listing medications used, and names of physicians and next of kin. Members complete a review form annually so that information on file can be updated if necessary. No charge is made for the update unless a new tag is needed.

For more information and/or application forms, write to Canadian Medic Alert Foundation, P.O. Box 9800, Don Mills, Ontario M3C 9Z9, or dial its toll-free number: 1–800–668–1507.

Med-I-Pant Inc. markets a line of Priva incontinence care products. All are washable and hence reusable, and made of natural cotton fabrics that allow the skin to breathe and promote good skin care. The line includes three-layer quilted bed pads; ultra-fit absorbent briefs with elastic at legs and snap closures, giving protection for heavy incontinence; acti-fit absorbent briefs, giving protection for moderate incontinence; and slim-fit shields for light incontinence.

For more information on the complete Priva product line, write Med-I-Pant at 4100 Parthenais, Montreal, Quebec H2K 3T9.

Motion 2000 distributes a line of walkers, along with an array of accessories to customize the devices. The Prisma has a basket designed to carry heavy loads. Options include a locking brake and a wide seat for comfortable sitting. The Primo has a shorter wheel base than the Prisma, allowing it to be turned in tighter spaces. It is also lighter and narrower. The Opal is a lightweight walker with an easily removable seat. Its handles point forward, encouraging better user posture. All three walkers have a locking mechanism so that they will not fold in use. Accessories include a cane holder, a waterproof bag, a one-hand brake, and a step-on curb climber.

For more information, write the company at 23 Railside Road, Unit 1, Toronto, Ontario M3A 1B2, or 11538 132 Street, Suite 104, Surrey, British Columbia V3R 7S2.

Newman Engineering Inc. manufactures the Uplift, a device which converts any chair with arms (including a wheelchair) into an automatic lifting chair for those who have difficulty sitting down or rising. Where other chairlifts tilt forward so that users more or less slide up or down, the Uplift supports a user on a horizontal surface that does not tilt. Anyone weighing between 80 and 240 pounds can use the Uplift.

For more information, write the company at 61 Research Road, Toronto, Ontario M4G 2G8.

Obus Forme Ltd. manufactures a lightweight, portable back brace that conforms to the shape of the back and provides firm support. It can be used in a regular chair, in an automobile seat, or in a wheelchair. Its covers are easily cleaned and are non-allergenic. Available too is a lumbar pad to provide support where it is most needed, and a seat which contours to the buttocks and relieves lumbar and thoracic fatigue. The seat is especially suited for use in wheelchairs with sling seats, which offer little in the way of support.

For more information, contact the company at 550 Hopewell Avenue, Toronto, Ontario M6E 2S6.

Parsons A.D.L. Inc. manufactures and/or distributes a wide variety of products, among them a walker which is also a shopping buggy and seat; a walker with a tray that has recesses for crockery and cutlery; reachers with magnets on their tips for picking up metal items such as pins; bath benches, boards, and safety handles; cutlery for those with impaired hand function, perhaps due to arthritis; and wheelchair arm pouches, trays, and other accessories.

For more information, contact the company at RR#4, Tottenham, Ontario L0G 1W0, or dial its toll-free number, 1-800-263-1281, from anywhere in Canada.

Robertson Custom Elevators designs and manufactures specialized elevators for easy upper-level access by people with disabilities. There are two designs. The TranCend 1000 has an enclosed grey melamine car, a platform size of 36 x 54 inches, and a speed of 20 feet per minute. The TranCend 2000 has an enclosed unfinished oak or birch car, a platform size of 36 x 48 inches, and a speed of 30 feet per minute. Both have hydraulic drive, door safety interlocks, and telephone jacks.

For more information, write the company at 1734 Orangebrook Court, Unit 9, Pickering, Ontario L1W 3G8.

Roloke Co. manufactures the Wal-Pil-O, a pillow that is, in fact, four pillows in one, since it has one wide and one narrow firm outer edge, and one soft and one medium centre section. The borders give good support to a user's neck, and he or she has a choice of centres to cradle the head. The pillow is made of non-allergenic polyester fibre and polyurethane. The company also makes the travelling Wal-Pil-O, a compact version that fits easily into a suitcase for travel by plane, car, or camper.

For more information, write the company at 5760 Hannum Avenue, Culver City, California, U.S.A., 90230.

Sancella Inc. distributes the Benefits pad and pant system to combat urinary incontinence in males. This two-part system combines highly absorbent pads and washable pants. The pads come in a range of four sizes: the smallest is to protect from light levels of incontinence, while the largest is worn through the night to provide long-lasting protection from even heavy incontinence.

For more information, write the company at 2300 Bristol Circle, Unit 6, Oakville, Ontario L6H 5X1.

Spenco Medical Corporation markets a wide range of products, among them arch and heel supports and other foot care items; hypo-allergenic warming supports for joints; an arthritis mitt which provides moist penetrating heat to the joints and muscles of the hand; wheelchair padding; seat, elbow, and foot pillows; a polymer wheelchair cushion; and crutch and wheelchair gloves.

For more information, write the company at P.O. Box 2501, Waco, Texas, U.S.A., 76702, or call its toll-free number, 1–800–387–9538, from anywhere in Canada.

Thera-P-Cushion Inc. makes the Thera-P-Support Cradle Pillow which has a raised area to support the neck—or jaw if the user is sleeping on her or his side. It gives relief to people who suffer from tension or neck or back pain by helping establish correct posture during sleep. It also makes the Thera-P-Back Cushion, which provides support for either back or neck, and the Thera-P-Footrest, which elevates the feet and positions them in such a way that the user's spine is aligned to ease back pain. As well, it makes the Thera-P-Body Pack, a compress which can be heated in a microwave oven or chilled in a freezer before being placed in a zippered outer case made of washable fabric and applied to the body to provide relief wherever needed.

For more information, write to the company at 331

Bowes Road, Unit 1, Concord, Ontario L4K 1J2, or call its toll-free number, 1–800–567–9926, from anywhere in Canada.

J.W. WESTMAN INC. distributes a wide range of Lumex products, among them grab bars and bathtub safety rails, bath seats, raised toilet seats, wheelchairs, canes, walkers, crutches, commodes, beds, bedrails, overbed tables, mattresses, pressure-management cushions, rockers, recliners, and kitchen, dressing, and grooming aids.

For more information, contact the company at 2485 Milltower Court, Mississauga, Ontario L5N 5Z6, or call its toll-free number, 1–800–387–8204, from anywhere in Canada.

RETAILERS

Several chains are big retailers of assistive aids and devices. One such is **Doncaster Home Health Care Centres**. Its head office and main location is at 224 Lesmill Road, Don Mills, Ontario M3B 2TS. The chain has other locations in British Columbia (Vancouver and Victoria), Nova Scotia (Dartmouth), Quebec (Greenfield Park and Montreal), and Ontario (Belleville, Brampton, Burlington, Etobicoke, Hamilton, Kingston, Kitchener, London, Markham, Mississauga, North Bay,

Orillia, Oshawa, Peterborough, St. Catharines, Sault Ste. Marie, Scarborough, Sudbury [two], and Windsor).

Another chain operation is **Shoppers Drug Mart Home Health Care Centres**. They are located in:

New Brunswick: 325 Vanier Boulevard, Bathurst; 1015 Regent Street, Fredericton; Moncton Medical Clinic, Moncton.

Nova Scotia: 176 Portland Street, Dartmouth; 5595 Fenwick Street, Halifax; Mayflower Mall, Grand Lake Road, Sydney.

Ontario: 20 Bellfarm Road, Barrie; Roseland Plaza, New Street, Burlington; Bathurst Medical Centre, 4256 Bathurst Street, Downsview; 90 Main Street, Dundas; Lakeview Plaza, Hwy #17 West, Kenora; 74 Kent Street West, Lindsay; 6855 Meadowvale Town Centre, Mississauga; Fairlawn Plaza, Carling Avenue, Ottawa; Cambrian Mall, Great Northern Road, Sault Ste. Marie; 685 McCowan Road, Scarborough; 285 Memorial Avenue, Thunder Bay; 70 Algonquin Boulevard West, Timmins; Main Square, 2615 Danforth Avenue, Toronto; 1100 Sheppard Avenue East, Willowdale.

Prince Edward Island: Oak Tree Place, 420 Queen Street, Charlottetown.

Sears Canada Inc. carries quite a wide range of assistive devices. These are no longer listed in the company's regular catalogue; instead, they appear in a separate publication. Ask the Customer Service Department of your local store for a copy of the "Sears Healthcare" catalogue.

Lawtons Drugs is a smaller Atlantic Canadian chain. It has outlets in Nova Scotia (Antigonish, Halifax, and Truro), New Brunswick (Moncton), Newfoundland (St. John's), and Prince Edward Island (Charlottetown).

AccessAbles runs a catalogue mail-order operation in Halifax. It supplies quite a range of aids, among them walkers, special cutlery, magnifiers, and non-slip mats. The company's address is 1540 Edward Street, Halifax, Nova Scotia B3H 3H7. The products it retails are also available at Woodlawn Surgical Appliances in Dartmouth; McQuinn's Drug and Harding Medical Supplies, both in Halifax; and MacQuarrie's Drug Mart in Truro.

Here's a short list of other outlets known to sell assistive aids and devices:

Alberta

H & H Care Ltd. and Home Care Medical Supply Centre, both in Calgary; Healthcare & Rehab Specialties in Edmonton.

British Columbia

B.C. Medical Equipment Ltd. and Lancaster Medical Supplies, both in Vancouver; and Anamed Medical Supplies and Surgical Supplies Ltd., both in Victoria.

Manitoba

Home Health Care Centre in Winnipeg.

New Brunswick

A.R. Menzies & Sons Ltd. in Fredericton; Wassons Pharmacy in Saint John.

Newfoundland

Medco Services Inc. in St. John's.

Northwest Territories

Northern Hospital Supplies in Whitehorse.

Nova Scotia

Harding Medical Supplies in Halifax

Ontario

Hunt's Convalescent Equipment Co. in Etobicoke; Therapy Supplies & Rental Ltd. in Mississauga and Toronto; Able Home Health Care in Toronto. The Sunnybrook Centre for Independent Living in Toronto carries a large range of products, and also designs and delivers various prosthetic devices, among them artificial ears, eyes, fingers, and other body parts, and orthotic devices (braces and splints). It also recommends wheelchair designs based on the user's need and condition, and custom-fabricates postural seating on site. As well, it runs one of the largest custom orthopaedic footwear services in this country. (A foot clinic staffed by an orthopaedic surgeon and a podiatry clinic staffed by podiatrists are held regularly at the centre.)

Prince Edward Island

Island Home Care and Ostomy Supplies in Charlottetown.

Quebec
Physio E.R.P. Ltd. in Montreal.
Saskatchewan
Independent Living, in Regina, and Total Independence Plus Inc. in Saskatoon.

To find other retailers of assistive aids and devices, look in your Yellow Pages under "Home Health Services & Supplies" and "Hospital Equipment & Supplies."

GRANTS AND LOANS

The Canadian Red Cross Society lends devices such as wheelchairs, walkers, crutches, canes, commodes, bath rails, patient lifts, back rests, and bedpans to convalescent people for periods of from one to three months. In some cases, a health care professional must recommend the loan. For more details, contact your local branch of the society.

Canada Mortgage and Housing Corporation's Home Adaptations for Seniors' Independence program helps those with low incomes pay for home adaptations. Grants go to those aged 65 or older who are homeowners or renters in the private market (renters must get written agreement from the landlord), who have difficulty with day-to-day activities because of diminishing abilities associated with aging, and who have a total household income below the limit for their area. (Contact the local CMHC office to find out what that limit is.) The adaptations should be minor ones, and should be permanent and fixed, although exceptions may be made for devices designed to give access to existing facilities, such as bath lifts. Qualifying modifications might be such items as grab bars, lever handles in place of knobs on doors, walk-in showers, bathtub seats, or easy-to-reach storage.

If a home requires extensive modifications—wider doorways and more space for a wheelchair user, perhaps—the owner may be able to obtain help from CMHC's Residential Rehabilitation Assistance Program. To qualify, household income must again be below the income ceiling for the area. Depending on the household income level, a forgivable loan may be made.

Veterans Affairs Canada also provides funds for home modifications for veterans aged 65 or older who have low incomes. Inquire at your local office.

(Incidentally, if you and your care receiver are not sure what home modifications might be the most effective, you might contact the Barrier-Free Design Centre, a non-profit organization providing information and consultation services on how to make facilities more accessible. The centre is located at 2075 Bayview Avenue, Toronto, Ontario M4N 3M5.)

The Canadian Association of Retired Persons (see Chapter 12 for more information on the association) has an arrangement whereby its members receive a 10 per cent discount when buying glasses from Standard Optical. Note that Standard flies under various names:

Eaton's Optical, countrywide; Braddock Optical, in Nova Scotia and Ontario; and Shorney's Optical, in Alberta, Manitoba, the Maritime provinces, Ontario, and Saskatchewan. As well, the association sells its members batteries for hearing aids at a discounted price.

Some branches of the War Amputations of Canada lend devices such as wheelchairs. Not all branches do so, however, so call your local branch to find out whether it has such a program. To find out if there is a branch near you, contact the head office at 2827 Riverside Drive, Ottawa, Ontario K1V 0C4.

Some members of the Canadian Rehabilitation Council for the Disabled lend assistive equipment. The following information is taken from the CRCD publication *Who, What, Where: A Directory of Services Provided by* CRCD *Members*. (If you would like a complete listing of CRCD members and the services they perform for people with disabilities, write for a copy of the directory to the CRCD, 45 Sheppard Avenue East, Suite 801, Toronto, Ontario M2N 5W9.)

- The Kinsmen Rehabilitation Foundation of British Columbia in Vancouver provides equipment on a no-charge permanent-loan basis. Equipment available includes bathroom and walking aids and portable communication aids.
- The Multiple Sclerosis Society of Canada in Toronto makes permanent loans of equipment or cost-shares

equipment purchases in areas where government funding is not available.

- The War Amputations of Canada in Ottawa gives amputees financial help in acquiring prosthetic needs. Travel and accommodation expenses incurred in visiting prosthetic centres may also be covered.
- The Quebec March of Dimes for the Disabled makes loans of some devices, among them wheelchairs, hospital beds, and walking aids.

Almost all provincial and territorial governments provide some form of help with assistive aids and devices and/or home modification. Here are some highlights.

In **Alberta**, the Alberta Aids to Daily Living Program pays part of the cost of devices. Under its Seniors' Independent Living Program it helps low-income elderly homeowners with grants to repair or improve their homes. Under its Home Adaption Program it gives grants to modify homes for wheelchair access and to make changes which improve or provide security in the home. Under its Seniors' Emergency Medical Alert Program it gives low-income elderly renters grants to buy medical alert home units from approved agencies.

In **Manitoba**, those living in communities with a population of fewer than 2,500 who want to modify their homes to make them more accessible for someone with a disability should apply for a grant from Manitoba

Housing. (Those in larger communities should apply to the CMHC, as noted above.) Manitoba residents aged 65 or older can receive financial assistance from the Manitoba Health Services Commission when buying new glasses from an optometrist or optician. A Home Care Equipment Program allows elders to rent certain assistive aids and devices without charge.

In the **Northwest Territories**, grants are available to people aged 60 or older who want to improve or renovate their homes.

In **Nova Scotia**, elders with low incomes can receive loans forgiven over time (the longer the ownership, the lower the repayment) to make repairs to their homes. At any age, homeowners with low incomes can receive one-time grants to have emergency repairs made. Help is also given to those who need to modify homes to make them wheelchair accessible.

The Assistive Devices Program in **Ontario** gives help to residents of the province who need certain devices. The program will pay up to 75 per cent of the cost of wheelchairs; seating inserts for wheelchairs; mobility aids such as walkers; ostomy supplies; prosthetic devices, including artificial limbs, eyes, and breasts; and respiratory equipment such as compressors, suction machines, and tracheotomy tubes. Loans are made to families with incomes below a certain level who need to make their homes more accessible for elderly and/or disabled family members. Depending on how long the family remains in the home, some of the loan may be forgiven. The longer the stay, the lower the repayment.

Prince Edward Island has a program that provides grants to elders on welfare who must make emergency repairs to their homes, and another program providing grants for materials used in home repairs or improvements.

In **Saskatchewan**, the Community Services Housing Division makes grants to those who must modify homes to make them accessible to people with physical disabilities. The lower the household income, the larger the grant. Through various programs, those with disabilities may be supplied with equipment and other items which help them remain in their own homes. Items available include ambulatory and mobility aids, respiratory aids, prosthetic and orthotic appliances and aids needed by the legally blind. Disabled people may also receive assistance when buying medical supplies, certain medications, and oxygen.

Enfranchised members of the Canadian Rehabilitation Council for the Disabled will provide funding over and above that available from provincial government sources for the purchase of aids and devices. These organizations are as follows:

Alberta

The Easter Seal Ability Council, Edmonton.

British Columbia

The Kinsmen Rehabilitation Foundation of British Columbia, Vancouver.

Manitoba

The Society for Manitobans with Disabilities Inc., Winnipeg.

New Brunswick

The Canadian Rehabilitation Council for the Disabled, New Brunswick Branch, Inc., Fredericton.

Newfoundland

The Newfoundland Society for the Physically Disabled, St. John's.

Nova Scotia

The Abilities Foundation of Nova Scotia, Halifax.

Ontario

The Ontario March of Dimes, Toronto.

Prince Edward Island

The P.E.I. Rehabilitation Council, Charlottetown.

Quebec

Quebec March of Dimes for the Disabled, Montreal.

Saskatchewan

Saskatchewan Abilities Council, Saskatoon.

CHAPTER EIGHT

LINKS THAT MAY SAVE LIVES

PEOPLE HAVE GONE INTO PERMANENT CARE because, living alone, they feared falling or having some other kind of accident or attack and perhaps dying because no one would come to help them. Such drastic action is now no longer necessary in many parts of the country, as devices, systems, and programs come into being to link those who live alone to the outside world. Here's a look at some of these links, starting with those that are national.

Letter Carrier Alert, a program available in Manitoba (Winnipeg and other communities), Ontario (York Division of Greater Metropolitan Toronto), Prince Edward Island (Charlottetown), Quebec (Montreal), and Yukon (Whitehorse), has letter carriers watch the homes of those who have signed up for it, looking for any indication that all is not well—for example, mail and newspapers not taken in, snow not cleared, and curtains not drawn back. If the letter carrier gets no response after knocking or ringing the door bell, he or she calls the centre that has the client's card on file. Coordinators at the centre then call the contact people listed on the client's card and ask that someone check on the client.

In Manitoba, you may obtain a card from any post office, or call 944–8555 and ask that a card be sent to you. In Ontario, your letter carrier will give you an application to enrol in the program. In Prince Edward Island, the program is called Postal Security Alert, and you may enrol by contacting either the PSA Coordinator, Letter Carrier Section, Charlottetown Post Office, Charlottetown, Prince Edward Island C1A 4A0, or Letter Carrier Alert, P.O. Box 285, Summerside, Prince Edward Island C1N 4Y8. In Montreal where the program is called Letter Carrier Watch, you may arrange for service by contacting your local post office. In Yukon, you can enrol by contacting the Seniors Information Centre, 106 Main Street, Suite 3, Whitehorse, Yukon Y1A 2A8.

Lifecall of Canada has an emergency response system. Users wear a waterproof help button (which need not be removed when bathing or showering) on the wrist like a watch, or attached to a belt. One press of the button puts the user in voice communication with the Lifecall Response Centre, where a trained communicator will ascertain the problem, at the same time looking up the user's personal and medical file, then summon the appropriate help. The service is available to anyone who lives in Ontario.

For more information, write to the company at 121 Willowdale Avenue, Unit 100, Willowdale, Ontario M2N 9Z9, or you may dial its toll-free number, 1-800-387-2966, from anywhere in Ontario.

Care Plus, a newly established division of Lifecall, makes the same service available through non-profit organizations across Canada. For more information, dial toll-free 1-800-661-2178 from anywhere in Canada.

Medic-Alarm (Canada) Ltd. also has an emergency response system. In this case, a press of the button alerts company staff who then try to reach people on a prearranged list—family members, friends, or neighbours perhaps. If they receive no replies, or if respondents say an ambulance is needed, staff also place the call to the ambulance service.

For more information, contact the company at 20 Bloor Street East, Toronto, Ontario M4Y 2B5.

Now here's a province-by-province look at some links that are not available nationally.

Alberta

Emergency Aid

Elderly people who have low incomes and live in rented accommodation can receive grants to help them buy a medical alert system from an approved agency. The system comprises a small portable transmitter, usually worn around the neck or on the wrist, and a base station, about the size of a large telephone directory, which usually is placed beside or beneath a telephone. The user simply presses a button on the transmitter to call for help.

Recipients of grants must be aged 65 or older, or aged 55 or older if widowed. They must have rented accommodation in the province for at least nine months in a year, must be Canadian citizens or landed immigrants, and must have lived for at least one year in Alberta and at least three years in Canada.

For more information, contact Seniors' Emergency Medical Alert Program, Housing Division, Alberta Municipal Affairs, P.O. Box 3040, Edmonton, Alberta T5J 4L7.

Manitoba

Around-the-Clock Protection

Victoria Lifeline is an around-the-clock, non-profit service operating in Winnipeg and surrounding communities. Clients are equipped with a portable help button; one press alerts the Response Centre at Victoria General Hospital. The service is operated by the hospital's research foundation, and is offered for a low monthly fee. No equipment purchase is required.

For further information, you may contact Victoria Lifeline, 2340 Pembina Highway, Winnipeg, Manitoba R3T 2E8.

A similar service is the Luther Home Personal Emergency Response System, which also provides 24-hour protection for elderly and/or disabled people.

For further information, contact Luther Home, 1081 Andrews Street, Winnipeg, Manitoba R2V 2G9.

Newfoundland

Emergency Help

Here's another Lifeline service, enabling elderly people who are in difficulty to call in help. The communication device this program uses is waterproof, so need not be removed while the user is bathing or showering. It also allows two-way voice communication. The service is sponsored by the Rotary Club.

For more information, contact the Emergency Alert Foundation, P.O. Box 2133, Station C, St. John's, Newfoundland A1C 5R6.

Nova Scotia

Reassurance by Phone

Telecare is a reassurance-by-telephone service operated by Northwood Homecare Ltd., a non-profit homecare service in Halifax. Elders who sign up pay no charge whatsoever. They are given special numbers to call at designated times each morning. Those at the other end of the line are volunteers. If they do not receive a call from one of the subscribers, they call one of two contacts the subscriber has listed. The contact will then be asked to run a check in case the subscriber has a problem of some kind.

For more information, write to Telecare, c/o Northwoodcare Inc., 2615 Northwood Terrace, Halifax, Nova Scotia B3K 3S5.

Ontario

When They're Calling You

Calling for You is a personal monitoring service that makes telephone checks on elderly people, the housebound, and children at home alone. It started in Metro Toronto, and quickly expanded into Burlington, Guelph, Hamilton, Kitchener-Waterloo, London, Niagara Falls, Oakville, and St. Catharines. The service works on any touch-tone phone. Clients can receive from one to ten calls daily to check that they are all right or perhaps to remind them to take medications. If clients do not reply by touching a button on their telephones, the service automatically alerts contacts on a predetermined list, who will then make their own checks.

For more information, write to Calling for You at 3266 Yonge Street, Suite 1411, Toronto, Ontario M4N 3P6, or, if calling from the Metro Toronto area, dial 440-4290, and from anywhere else in the province, dial toll-free 1-800-463-0405.

Good Neighbours

The aim of Good Neighbours is to have people in the district reach out and help each other. Perhaps someone across the street notices that an elder's drapes have not been drawn back and the newspaper has not been taken in; he or she will then cross the street and try to find out if anything is wrong. Perhaps a janitor in an apartment block offers to change a light bulb for an older person so he or she won't have to climb up on a chair or carry out some other risky manoeuvre. As well, volunteers staff a 24-hour telephone answering service. Someone who has a problem may call in. So may the neighbour who notices no one is up and about in the house across the street. The volunteer then makes a call to whomever seems appropriate—perhaps a relative, the ambulance service, or the health department.

So far, the Good Neighbours concept has not spread beyond Ontario, but it would be surprising if it did not do so sooner or later. At time of writing, the program existed in the following communities: Acton, Alliston, Barrie, Beeton, Brampton, Brantford, Burlington, Cambridge, Chatham, Durham and Southwest Grey Area, Eagle River, Elliot Lake, Fort Frances, Halton Hills, Hanover, Hornings Mills, Ingersoll, Kapuskasing, Kemptville, Kincardine, Kingsville and Gosfield Twsp., Kitchener, Leamington and Mersea Twsp., Meaford, Milton, Minnitaki, Newcastle, New Tecumseth, North Toronto, Oakville, Oshawa, Owen Sound, Peterborough, Sudbury, Thornbury and Area, Thunder Bay, Tottenham, Vermilion Bay, Waterloo, Wheatley and Romney Twsp., Whitby, and Windsor.

For more information, write to Good Neighbours, c/o Office for Seniors' Issues, Education Resources Unit, 76 College Street, Toronto, Ontario M7A 1N3.

Ontario Blue Cross Lifeline

This service is available to all residents of Ontario. A subscriber wears a small waterproof personal help button, and a voice unit is connected to the telephone jack. If the subscriber presses the button, she or he is immediately connected by voice to a monitor at Blue Cross. If the monitor hears no reply, he or she notifies contact personnel—for example, family members living in the vicinity or neighbours—previously named by the subscriber. This system has an added feature: an inactivity alarm alerts Blue Cross monitors if the subscriber has been unusually inactive for either 12 or 24 hours (either period can be selected).

For more information, contact Ontario Blue Cross at 150 Ferrand Drive, Toronto, Ontario M3C 1H6, or dial its toll-free number, 1-800-361-7161, from anywhere in Ontario.

Prince Edward Island

Emergency Response Systems and Devices

In Prince Edward Island, the Lifeline service is made available by the Hillsborough Rotary Club. If you would like more information, contact the Queen Elizabeth Hospital on Riverside Drive in Charlottetown and ask for someone involved with the Lifeline program.

The Main Street Messenger is an emergency response device consisting of a telephone and an alert button set in a pendant, which the user presses to summon help.

For more information, contact P.E.I. Alert Inc., P.O. Box 2991, Charlottetown, P.E.I. C1A 8C5.

Quebec

Security System

Here is yet another 24-hour Lifeline service. In this one, activating the portable alarm, worn as a bracelet or necklace, alerts trained staff at the Royal Victoria Hospital in Montreal. Subscribers to the service pay a fee, but if someone cannot afford the fee, special arrangements will be made.

For more information, contact the Royal Victoria Hospital.

CHAPTER NINE
HOUSING CHOICES

AS NOTED IN THE INTRODUCTION, WE CANADIANS "warehouse" our elders—in other words, help them into permanent-care establishments—at far too high a rate. As also mentioned earlier, the main reason this book exists is to help caregivers find the services, programs, and other forms of assistance they need to ensure their elders remain in the community at large.

But even if caregivers and/or elders utilize such services and programs to the full, the day may come when independent living is no longer possible, and the elder must opt for the security of some form of shared or sheltered accommodation.

VARIOUS FORMS OF ALTERNATIVE ACCOMMODATION

Unless you have already had occasion to find alternative living arrangements for an elderly person, you may well be unaware of all the numerous forms of shared or sheltered accommodation that exist. So, before you learn how to find them, here's a rundown of those various forms.

Homesharing. Here, two people—the home provider and the sharer—live in the same house. At Sharing, a Toronto agency that matches people aged 55 or older with others of whatever age, staff generally find such situations work out best when sharers are of different generations. Needless to say, matching services carefully check the credentials of those wishing to share, and attempt to achieve arrangements that will be lasting.

Garden Suites. Also known as granny flats, these are small, prefabricated, portable homes. They are brought in and set down on a foundation in the backyard of an existing home, probably a son's or a daughter's. When no longer needed, the homes are simply removed.

The benefits of garden suites are obvious. Occupants of both the suite and the main house can have as much or as little privacy as they want, while the occupant of the suite has the pleasure and security of having family members nearby.

Unfortunately, many municipalities have bylaws that do not permit the erection of a second building on one lot. But, in time, as the population ages and as pressures on appropriate housing increase, this situation will probably change.

Accessory Apartments. These self-contained living spaces are generally created in a caregiver's home for an elderly parent or other relative. All that may be necessary is the addition of a kitchen and perhaps walls and doors, provided the house already has at least two bathrooms.

Here again, many municipal bylaws mandate against the creation of accessory apartments—a situation that may well change in the fullness of time.

Life Lease Communities. Most of these are in the form of highrise apartments. Residents pay both a fairly substantial amount on moving in and monthly fees to cover the expenses of running the community. Many sponsors are non-profit or religious groups, meaning residents get a good deal: if the actual cost of a unit is $100,000, say, and the market value is $125,000, the resident would pay $100,000 to move in.

Residents who move in, then later find they need some specialized care, such as nursing assistance, can usually receive care in return for extra fees. Usually, too, if residents want to leave—perhaps to go into permanent care—they receive a refund of a portion of their lump-sum down payment.

Life Tenancy Communities. These are almost identical to life lease communities. There are just two differences: the size of the down payment is partially based on age and gender—younger residents and women, both of whom are expected to live longer, pay more—and, if a resident leaves, there may be only a small refund or none at all.

Shared Equity Communities. In these, residents buy a portion of the equity in their units (generally anywhere from 25 to 75 per cent), and pay rent for that portion retained by the community's developer. Residents also pay maintenance fees. They can sell their shares in their units—in some cases to the community's developer or operator, in others to anyone they like. Anyone contemplating this form of retirement living should ask about reimbursement if they must sell to the developer or operator; the price they receive may not be too generous.

Loan Stock Communities. Residents here make interest-free loans to the community's sponsor and in return are permitted to live in their units rent free for the rest of their lives. If they leave, the sponsor repays the loan. If they die, the sponsor repays the loan to the estate. Anyone contemplating this kind of arrangement should give consideration to the fact that he or she will not benefit from any increase in a unit's value.

Congregate Housing. This is designed in such a way that residents, individuals or couples, all have private quarters—usually small, self-contained apartments or private bed-sitting rooms which they furnish themselves. Dining rooms and lounges are shared communal spaces. Residents are provided with main meals. They typically pay fairly modest fees to cover mortgage payments, a housekeeper's wages, food, utilities, and repairs.

Foster Homes. These are suitable for older people who need no nursing care but can no longer live independently in their own homes. Foster home managers usually look after several tenants, who help with chores such as cleaning and dishwashing if they are able to do so, and who are encouraged to become friends with each other and go on outings together.

Retirement Communities. These may be villages comprising several hundred residences—bungalows, perhaps, or cottages or mobile homes—or subdivisions or clusters of townhouses. Some communities provide the barest minimum of services: lawn cutting and snow shovelling, perhaps. Others provide many services, among them homemaking, transportation, and personal care. Others again also provide ongoing help for those who have bought into the community but can now no longer live independently.

Retirement Apartments. These are rental units. As is the case with retirement communities, the level of services available—and hence the level of costs—varies. However, quite a number are operated by government or non-profit agencies, so rental fees at these ones are quite low. A few of these retirement apartments are adjacent to shopping malls; residents can thus shop without having to go outdoors.

Share-A-Bed Programs. Here, two part-time residents of a permanent-care facility share the use of a room. One of the two lives in it for three days in each week, returning to his or her own home for the other four days, during which the second person will move into the permanent-care facility. Users of the program enjoy the special care they receive as residents and also enjoy remaining very much in the community at large. Caregivers, in turn, welcome the several days of respite when the care receiver is in the facility and also have the pleasure of having him or her around for half the week.

Long-Term Care Facilities. Both government-operated or government-sponsored and private homes providing different levels of care have different names depending on which province they are in. For instance, in Ontario long-term care facilities are non-profit and are subsidized. Retirement homes and nursing homes are private, with the latter providing a higher level of care. In Manitoba, privately operated homes are known as residential care or personal care facilities, with the latter providing a greater level of care. In Prince Edward Island, community care facilities are privately owned and operated; the vast majority don't provide nursing care. Nursing homes, which provide nursing care, are also privately operated, but government may subsidize residents who can't afford the full rate. Manors are government-operated and provide nursing care; again those who can't afford to pay may be subsidized.

Your or your elder's family physician, staff at the local family service association, or a public health nurse can tell you what are the correct names for long-term care facilities in your province. They can also tell you what level of care would be suitable for your elder and where to find facilities providing that level of care in the district.

Also note that changes are in the wind. In Ontario, legislation has been enacted which will, over the long haul, see many levels of care provided at a single home, so that residents will not need to move from a home providing little or no nursing care to one providing much nursing care as their conditions deteriorate, but will be able to "age in place," as the catchphrase goes.

As well, as you learned in Chapter 1, those seeking

permanent-care facilities will need to knoc[illegible]
door—that of the placement coordination s[illegible]
in the district.

When the legislation is fully implemented, [illegible]erly person will be able to enter a permanent-care facility only by going through the PCS.

Continuing Care Retirement Communities. These communities provide a continuum of care, starting, perhaps, with a retirement complex, where little or no care is provided, and moving through minimum care facilities right up to a chronic care hospital. Thus those moving into these communities have the comforting guarantee that they will never need to make another move unless they choose so to do.

Two types of continuing care retirement communities exist. In one, all facilities are located on one campus, as is the case with the Baycrest Centre for Geriatric Care in Toronto and the Northwoodcare complex in Halifax, two centres that are widely recognized for their excellence.

In the other type, care is also provided along a continuum, but facilities are not located on one campus. One such exists in the municipality of Niagara, Ontario. There, a linked system comprises group homes, health care and recreational centres, retirement and nursing homes, and so on.

WHERE TO FIND ALTERNATIVE ACCOMMODATION

Sharing programs exist in quite a number of Ontario communities, but this form of accommodation does not seem to have caught on so strongly in other provinces so far. Programs in existence at the time of writing were:

Alberta: Edmonton, The Society for the Retired and Semi-Retired

Nova Scotia: Dartmouth, Dartmouth Share

Ontario: Brantford, Brant Homesharing; Hamilton, VON Homesharing; Kitchener, Lutherwood Youth Employment Centre; London, London Housing Registry; North Bay, LIPI Homesharing; North York, East York Flemingdon Housing Registry and North York Housing Connection; Ottawa, Ottawa YM-YWCA Homeshare and Match & Share; Peterborough, FCS Peterborough Homesharing; Scarborough, Scarborough Housing Help Centre; Sudbury, Homesharing—Sudbury; Thorold, Regional Niagara Homesharing; Toronto, City of Toronto Homesharing Program, Sharing, and York Housing Registry; Windsor, Windsor Homesharing

Quebec: Hull, Les Habitations Partagées de l'Outaouais Urbain; Jonquiere, Habitations Partagées de Saguenay; Montreal, Project co-existence, Catholic Community Services Inc.

Share-A-Bed programs are rare. It appears that only one care provider in Canada has such a program. The Capital Care Group, headquartered in Edmonton, Alberta, provides homecare in the Edmonton district and runs Share-A-Bed programs at its four permanent-care centres in Edmonton: Dickinsfield, Grandview, Lynnwood, and Norwood.

Many retirement homes and nursing homes are individually owned and operated. There are also "chain" operations in which one company owns and/or manages a number of homes.

One such company is Beacon Hill Lodges Inc. Beacon Hill has retirement homes in Cumberland, Hawkesbury, North Bay, Sudbury, and Timmins in Ontario, and Sherbrooke in Quebec. It has nursing homes in Victoria and West Vancouver, British Columbia; Winnipeg, Manitoba; and Bedford, Hamilton, Newmarket, Ottawa, Thunder Bay, and Windsor, Ontario.

For more information, contact Beacon Hill Lodges Inc., 195 The West Mall, Suite 600, Etobicoke, Ontario M9C 5K1.

Central Park Lodges also operates a large number of homes. It has retirement homes in Calgary, Alberta; St. Lambert, Quebec; and Brantford, East York, Hamilton, Kitchener, London, North York, Ottawa, Toronto, and Windsor, Ontario. It has nursing homes in Calgary, Edmonton, and Medicine Hat, Alberta; Victoria, British Columbia; Brandon and Winnipeg, Manitoba; and Kitchener, Thunder Bay, and Toronto, Ontario.

For more information, contact Central Park

Lodges, 1120 Finch Avenue West, 8th Floor, Downsview, Ontario M3J 3H7.

Diversicare also operates both retirement homes and nursing homes. It has retirement homes in Kelowna and Richmond, British Columbia; and Chatham, Delora, Leamington, London, Peterborough, St. Thomas, and Tilbury, Ontario. It has nursing homes in Brampton, Garson, Ingersoll, London, Mississauga, Scarborough, Streetsville, Tilbury, West Hill, and Willowdale, all in Ontario.

For more information, contact Diversicare Management Services, 2121 Argentia Road, Suite 301, Mississauga, Ontario L5N 2X4.

Extendicare operates mainly nursing homes, although it also runs retirement residences in Oakville and Willowdale, Ontario. In Alberta, it runs nursing homes in Athabasca, Bonnyville, Calgary (six), Edmonton (two), Fort Macleod, Leduc, Lethbridge, Mayerthorpe, St. Paul, Viking, and Vulcan. In British Columbia, it operates homes in Kamloops, Kelowna, and Victoria. Two homes in Manitoba are in Winnipeg. In Ontario, it operates homes in Cochrane, Gloucester, Gravenhurst, Haileybury, Haliburton, Hearst, Kapuskasing, Kingston, Kirkland Lake, London, Nepean, Newmarket, Northbrook, Oshawa, Ottawa (three), Peterborough, Port Stanley, St. Catharines, Sault Ste. Marie (two), Scarborough, Schumacher, Sudbury (two), West Hill, and Willowdale (two). In Saskatchewan, it runs homes in Moose Jaw, Regina (three), and Saskatoon.

For more information, contact Extendicare Health Services Inc., 3000 Steeles Avenue East, Suite 700, Markham, Ontario L3R 9W2.

In many cases, and especially if you are looking for regular retirement communities or those with varying financial options, such as life lease communities, you may find what you want by scanning the advertisements in some of the newspapers and magazines listed in Chapter 13 of this book.

The family physician may be able to tell you about various forms of alternative accommodation in the vicinity. Also contact the local health board, housing authority, and community information centre.

Staff at public libraries can probably direct you to listings of homes. Many libraries also have two comprehensive guides, *Directory of Long-Term Care Centres in Canada* and *Canadian Hospital Directory*. Both are published by the Canadian Hospital Association, and both are updated regularly.

Contact your provincial housing ministry. It may maintain a registry of retirement homes and lodges. It may also participate in providing low-cost housing for the elderly.

Contact your local office of the Canada Mortgage and Housing Corporation. CMHC launched pilot programs with garden suites and can tell you more about them. Sometimes CMHC teams up with other authorities to provide low-cost housing for elders.

Look in the Yellow Pages under "Retirement Communities and Homes."

Don't expect to find numerous foster homes right across Canada except in the province of Quebec, where they seem to be popular.

One organization providing congregate housing is the Abbeyfield Houses Society of Canada, headquartered in Toronto. Those living in an Abbeyfield House have private bed-sitting rooms, most of them with en-suite bathrooms. At the time of writing, there were seven Abbeyfield Houses in British Columbia, in Kelowna, Vancouver, and the Greater Victoria area, and three in Ontario, in Guelph, Port Hope, and Toronto. The society plans to open more—in Golden, Kelowna, Vancouver, Vernon, and Victoria in British Columbia, and in Ottawa and Peterborough in Ontario.

For more information, contact the society at 4120 Yonge Street, Toronto, Ontario M2P 2B8.

FINAL THOUGHTS ON THE TOPIC

The decision to change living arrangements is seldom made easily. Here are two considerations you and your care receiver should perhaps bear in mind.

Finding and working with a counsellor who is knowledgeable about different living arrangements could lead to a better decision. Where might you find such a counsellor? You might try the local VON Canada operation; VON personnel are generally highly knowledgeable and skilled at working efficiently with older people. A public health nurse might be a good counsellor. So might a social worker in a geriatric centre or a family service association, or a social worker or a discharge planning coordinator in a nearby hospital.

Second, as was pointed out in Chapter 3, having the best professional qualifications in the world cannot compensate for poor delivery of service. There can surely be few people who have not read in newspapers or magazines, or heard or seen on radio or television, reports of poor conditions and poor treatment experienced at permanent-care facilities.

How do you recognize a good facility? Regardless of where you live, you would be well advised to obtain a copy of "Nursing Home Checklist," a nine-page pamphlet prepared by an organization called Concerned Friends of Ontario Citizens in Care Facilities. It contains a questionnaire to be filled out when visiting and inspecting a permanent care facility. The organization will send you (wherever you live) a copy on receipt of $5, to cover shipping and handling charges. Its address is P.O. Box 1054, Station Q, Toronto, Ontario M4T 2P2.

And, as we counselled in Chapter 3, ask around. Canvass anyone you know or have heard of who has relatives or friends in foster homes, congregate housing, retirement homes, whatever, noting the facilities that are given praise and those that are cited with a warning. A visit to a seniors' club or two might yield valuable information; members quite likely have relatives or friends in shared or sheltered accommodation and will thus be good sources.

A final tip. If you are looking for a permanent-care facility of some kind, you may do well to avoid those with plenty of vacancies at all times (not a good sign), and instead concentrate on those that have waiting lists.

CHAPTER TEN

A CORNUCOPIA OF CARE

BECAUSE OUR POPULATION IS AGING, MANY NEW AND often innovative services and programs for elders, and for those with physiological or psychological disabilities, are coming into being. As well, our store of knowledge as to how to keep people well and young at heart in later life is increasing.

In this chapter, we'll take a look at some useful services and programs, and at several practices that promote good health. Some of the programs and services are pilot projects, and others are not yet widely available. But all are of interest.

Here, first, are services, programs, and developments available nationwide.

St. John Ambulance Courses

At least four St. John Ambulance courses will be of interest to older people and to caregivers.

One is "Family Health Care," in which participants

learn how to care for an ill or convalescent person at home, in 17 hour-long sessions.

Another is "Healthy Aging." This shows older people ways in which they can continue living independent, healthy, and productive lives, in 10 hour-long sessions.

A third is "Caring for the Aging," which teaches caregivers basic nursing skills to help them look after elderly people at home, in 20 hour-long sessions.

The fourth is "Level-A Heart Saver," in which participants learn to perform cardiopulmonary resuscitation and anti-choking manoeuvres, in six hour-long sessions.

Obtain details from your local St. John Ambulance branch. To find out whether there is a branch in your area, contact your provincial or territorial headquarters. These are located in Alberta (Edmonton), British Columbia (Vancouver), Manitoba (Winnipeg), New Brunswick (Fredericton), Newfoundland (St. John's), Northwest Territories (Yellowknife), Nova Scotia (Dartmouth), Ontario (Toronto), Prince Edward Island (Charlottetown), Quebec (Montreal), and Saskatchewan (Regina).

Fun & Fitness

The Canadian Red Cross Society organizes Fun & Fitness in the '90s classes at some but not all of its branches. These are light exercise programs designed for healthy but inactive older people. The programs encourage participants to increase their level of physical activity. As well, participants have a chance to meet new people, and to have fun. Classes are held once a week and run by volunteer instructors who are trained and certified by the society. Exercises are designed to improve general health, strength, circulation, posture, and digestion; to promote relaxation; to maintain suppleness; and to increase heart and lung capacity, and energy levels.

For more information, contact your local branch of the society.

Safety First

The RCMP and local police forces counsel older individuals, both singly and in groups, on how to avoid becoming crime statistics. They will also come to your home and counsel you on how to make it more secure and entryproof.

For more information, contact your local RCMP detachment or police station.

Walking Campaign

The National Walking Campaign is designed to start people, and especially those aged 50 or older, on walking programs, and to give them information on walking. The campaign began in 1990 as a three-year project and was winding down at the time of writing. However, indications are that the program will continue, either under its original name or under the name "Active Living," operating out of the same address (see below).

Contact the campaign if you would like information on how to lead a walking program, advice on starting a walking program, either alone or with a companion or companions, or counsel on how to add challenge to your existing walking program. The campaign also has a useful booklet covering such topics as safety tips for walkers, monitoring heart rate to chart physical improvement, stretching exercises to condition major leg muscles used during walking, and walking programs designed to increase the number and duration of walks on a weekly basis.

An offshoot of the campaign is a national project called Go For Green, which encourages environmental friendliness. Participation in the project can take many forms. For instance, if you are a member of a walking club, you might urge the club to "adopt" a walking trail, then keep that trail litter-free at all times. Or if your group walks in a park, you might ask a park interpreter to walk along on the next outing and tell members about the ecosystem they are travelling through. If you want tips on how to make your walks environmentally friendly, or if you have tips to share with others, write in.

For information on both the National Walking Campaign and Go For Green, write to 1600 James Naismith Drive, Suite 312, Gloucester, Ontario K1B 5N4, or dial toll-free 1-800-361-2756.

New Horizons: A Source of Funding

If you and/or an elder you know want to start up a project involving groups of elders and retirees working together for their own benefit, or for the benefit of others in the community, you may wish to apply to the federal government's New Horizons program for funding.

Funds are available to start new activities, or expand and build upon existing ones. Contributions typically cover 18 months, at the end of which time groups are expected to do their own fundraising, be it through membership dues, various events, donations, or support from the community.

New Horizons projects are extremely diverse. Grants have been made to many organizations, among them ones starting up sporting activities, community services, arts and crafts groups, and recreational activities.

For more information, contact the New Horizons office responsible for your province or territory. Offices are located in Alberta, the Northwest Territories, and Yukon (Edmonton), British Columbia (Vancouver), Manitoba (Winnipeg), New Brunswick (Moncton), Newfoundland (St. John's), Nova Scotia (Halifax), Ontario (Toronto), Prince Edward Island (Charlottetown),

Quebec (Montreal), and Saskatchewan (Regina). There are also two sub-offices you may contact: one is in Quebec City, the other in Kitchener, Ontario.

Independence Program: Another Funding Source

The Seniors Independence Program is another federal initiative. Its aim is to encourage older people to become involved in projects that promote independence and improve their quality of life, to foster self-care and mutual-help activities among the elderly, and to help increase resources that promote the health, education, and social welfare of elders. Community-based projects emphasizing elders' involvement are of great interest.

Community groups and other voluntary, non-governmental, non-profit groups may apply for funding, which will last for a period of up to three years.

For more information, contact your regional office. (You will find it in the Government of Canada section of your phone directory's blue pages, among the Health and Welfare listings.) Regional offices are located in Alberta, the Northwest Territories, and Yukon (Edmonton), British Columbia (Vancouver), Manitoba (Winnipeg), New Brunswick (Moncton), Newfoundland (St. John's), Nova Scotia (Halifax), Ontario (Toronto), Prince Edward Island (Charlottetown), Quebec (Montreal), and Saskatchewan (Regina).

Chrysler Helps Disabled Drivers

The Chrysler Canada Physically Challenged Program gives qualified applicants cash allowances of up to $500 (that's over and above existing factory discounts, which are rebates offered by manufacturers when they want to increase sales of certain models), to help them modify Chrysler vehicles to make them suitable for disabled drivers or passengers.

Modifications may be special hand controls, for instance, or a hoist to make the vehicle wheelchair accessible.

For more details, contact your local Chrysler dealer, or call toll-free 1–800–255–9877.

Hear All About It! Listen to VoicePrint

VoicePrint: The National Broadcast Reading Service has been described as "an audio newsstand." It features around-the-clock readings seven days a week from newspapers, magazines, newsletters, and books. Its audience comprises people who are visually impaired and who thus had no direct access to the news or to feature material until VoicePrint launched in December 1990.

VoicePrint is transmitted by cable television companies, most commonly as an audio feed on an alphanumeric channel. So for those who do not now have cable connections, the only cost to receive VoicePrint is that of cable service. And since a year's cable service costs about as much as a year's subscription to one metropolitan newspaper and one magazine, the outlay buys great value because listeners hear readings from not just two but dozens of publications.

Cable companies in all the provinces now broadcast VoicePrint, and people in almost five million homes listen to the service.

To find out whether it is available in your area, and, if so, on what channel, call your local cable company. If you do not receive satisfaction, write to VoicePrint at P.O. Box 1728, Station R, Toronto, Ontario M4G 4A3.

Fitting Fashions

Silvert's Clothing for Seniors is a multiple-access retail business operating out of Concord, Ontario. It runs a shop-at-home service for those who can't get out, which is available in every province. It runs a mail order business, distributing about 20,000 catalogues seasonally. In the Toronto area, five mobile shops on wheels visit long-term care facilities for the elderly. And it operates a regular storefront business in Concord. Garments, for both women and men, have larger-than-average buttons, and easy-to-handle fastenings such as snaps or Velcro. Prices are reasonable. If a shop-at-home buyer spends less than $100, the company imposes a $25 service charge—something it has not yet had to do, however.

For more information and/or to obtain a catalogue, write the company at 3280 Steeles Avenue West, Concord, Ontario L4K 2Y2, or dial toll-free 1-800-387-7088 from anywhere in Canada.

Telephone Pioneers

Telephone Pioneers is a national organization with some 80,000 members, all of whom have been employees of Bell Canada or other telephone companies for 15 years or more. They work with those who have some impairment: clients may themselves be members, or they may be individuals or organizations within the community.

Provided clients have a certificate signed by a medical practitioner, members will provide, free of charge, such items as large dial plates for telephones, touch-tone pads, and a repair service for talking books. They also help members in various other ways, perhaps by putting in ramps for those who are wheelchair-bound.

The organization has three chapters in Ontario, two in Quebec, and one in each of the other provinces. For more information, write the head office at 2920 Matheson Boulevard East, Mississauga, Ontario L4W 4M7.

Now, here's a province-by-province listing of some services and programs.

Alberta

Free Education

Anybody aged 65 or older can take part in a credit

course without charge, so long as space is available after fee-paying students have enrolled, at the Alberta Vocational College campuses at Calgary, Edmonton, Lac La Biche, and Lesser Slave Lake, at the Southern Alberta Institute of Technology in Calgary, and at the Northern Alberta Institute of Technology in Edmonton.

Some other educational institutions in the province may provide courses on a tuition-free basis, or for a minimal registration fee.

For more information, contact the registrar's office at colleges and universities in your area.

Lawyer Referral Service

Anyone who needs a lawyer but does not know one to turn to should contact the Law Society of Alberta's Lawyer Referral Service. He or she will be given the name of three lawyers, and will then receive the first 30 minutes of consultation free of charge, during which time fees will be discussed and the client will decide whether or not to retain the services of this lawyer.

For more information, contact Lawyer Referral Service Office, 919-11 Avenue S.W., Room 600, Calgary, Alberta T2R 1P3.

Sport and Recreation Group

The Alberta Senior Citizens Sport and Recreation Association is a volunteer action group. It promotes sport, recreation, and fitness development for those aged 55 and older. It encourages participation at the local level in the Alberta Seniors' Games. Members pay $10 a year, and in return receive a quarterly newsletter, sport accident insurance in the amount of $15,000, and regular communication of information about province-wide events.

For more information, contact Alberta Senior Citizens Sport and Recreation Association, 1520-4 Street S.W., Suite 890, Calgary, Alberta T2R 1H5.

British Columbia

Counsellors Program

The Ministry of Social Services appoints older people as volunteer Senior Citizen Counsellors, whose role is to help other seniors. Counsellors can put elderly people in touch with service agencies, assist in the completion of applications for pensions and other benefits, and furnish information on various programs, such as bus passes, housing for the elderly, and consumer services.

You can reach a counsellor by telephone. Call the local Ministry of Social Services district office, which is listed under "Governments—British Columbia" in the blue pages of your telephone directory.

Stroke Recovery Association of B.C.

The association comprises almost 40 stroke clubs across the province. Members are those who have had strokes and possibly their family members. Clubs hold workshops to help those who have had strokes to recover from their disabilities and generally regain their health.

For more information and/or to find out if there is a chapter near you, contact the association at 109-119 West Pender Street, Vancouver, British Columbia V6B 1S5.

Help for Substance Abusers

TRYLINE is a telephonic substance-abuse information and referral service, available around the clock, seven days a week. It is operated by the Ministry of Health and Ministry Responsible for Seniors, and directs callers to counselling and resources in their community.

The service is available to anyone in British Columbia. Its toll-free number is 1–800–663–1441.

Nutrition Counsel

The Ministry of Health's Nutrition Branch has a toll-free, province-wide resource line for use by anyone needing advice on nutrition. A dietitian will answer callers' questions: hence the program's name, Dial-A-Dietitian.

Callers in the Greater Vancouver area dial 732–9191. Those elsewhere in the province dial 1–800–667–3438.

Service for Wheelchair-Bound Renters

The British Columbia Housing Management Commission (BCHMC) maintains two registries, one of housing units in the Lower Mainland that are wheelchair accessible, the other of disabled people who are seeking such accommodation. BCHMC can thus match applicants with vacancies.

For more information, contact BCHMC at 4330 Kingsway, Suite 1701, Burnaby, British Columbia V5H 4G7.

Manitoba

Age and Opportunity

Age and Opportunity is a Winnipeg agency that provides retirement planning services to help individuals, couples, groups, and organizations. Issues covered include health, housing, financial security, pension and other benefits, legal affairs, psychological preparation for retirement, and awareness of the aging process. The organization maintains a library containing articles, books, studies, manuals, films, and videos on various aspects of retirement planning. It also operates six centres for elderly people in Winnipeg at which educational and recreational activities take place.

For more information, contact Age and Opportunity, 323 Portage Avenue, Suite 304, Winnipeg, Manitoba R3B 2C1.

Learning at Home

Homebound Learning Opportunities (HLO) is an educational outreach service for those aged 50 or older who are homebound, temporarily, seasonally, or permanently. It provides more than 120 course topics to choose from, either for a one-to-one learning experience or for group learning. It also has a 30-topic audio-visual lending library to complement the courses.

HLO also seeks to make creative use of homebound retirees' skills, knowledge, and experience; they may function as facilitators for other participants or make contact by telephone daily with other homebound people.

For more information, contact Homebound Learning Opportunities, c/o Creative Retirement Manitoba, 294 Portage Avenue, Suite 811, Winnipeg, Manitoba R3C 0B9.

Stroke Association of Manitoba

Those who have had strokes become members of this association—often soon after release from hospital—and take part in workshops offering physiotherapy and speech therapy training with the aim of recovering from their disabilities and regaining good health as soon as possible. As well, educational programs teach members about communicating after a stroke, and generally help those recovering also to regain their self-esteem. At the time of writing, chapters existed in Winnipeg, Dauphin, Flin Flon, and Steinbach, and many more were in the process of being established.

For more information, contact the association at 333 Vaughan Street, Suite 1, Winnipeg, Manitoba R3B 3J9.

Emergency Information

Should a homeowner lose consciousness and emergency helpers be called in, the latter can look at the refrigerator door to see whether there is a sticker indicating the presence of a K-Vial of Life attached to the underside of a shelf inside the refrigerator. Inside the vial is a form with information about the unconscious person, her or his medical condition, next of kin, family practitioner, and hospital.

K-Vials are distributed without charge by the Kiwanis and by ambulance services.

For more information, contact the Kiwanis Club of South Winnipeg, K-Vial, P.O. Box 485, St. Vital P.O., Winnipeg, Manitoba R2M 5C8.

Dentistry at Home

Patients who find it difficult or impossible to visit a regular dental clinic can avail themselves of an outreach program run by the University of Manitoba's Faculty of Dentistry. Using a dental mobile van, faculty dentists and hygienists provide a wide range of treatments in private homes, retirement homes, and hospitals. Examinations and written estimates of treatment cost are provided before treatment is begun.

For more information, contact the University of Manitoba Faculty of Dentistry, 777 McDermot Avenue, Winnipeg, Manitoba R3E 0T6.

Drug Counsel by Telephone

Most elders are on medications of one kind or another. Many know little about the drugs they take, and may not take them correctly. This is why the University of Manitoba's Faculty of Pharmacy has a Medication Information Line for the Elderly (MILE).

Those wanting information about the medications they or their care receivers are taking, including proper dosages, can call MILE Monday through Friday mornings. The service is province-wide; those living outside Winnipeg call toll-free 1–800–432–1960, extension 6493.

For more information, contact the Medication Information Line for the Elderly, Faculty of Pharmacy, Room 407, University of Manitoba, Winnipeg, Manitoba R3T 2N2.

Legal Services for Elders

Under the auspices of Legal Aid Manitoba, elderly people on a limited income can obtain legal services through Age and Opportunity. (See above, page 143, for more information on this organization.)

Elders wanting free or low-cost legal advice may also get in touch with the Manitoba Society of Seniors.

In each of the society's regions, lawyers are available who offer certain services at a low cost, as well as a 30-minute consultation without charge.

For more information, contact Manitoba Society of Seniors, 803 Somerset Place, 294 Portage Avenue, Winnipeg, Manitoba R3C 0B9.

New Brunswick

Self-Help Stroke Clubs

People who have had strokes can benefit from contact with others who have had the same experience. Similarly, those who have been paralysed following a stroke and members of their families can profit from contact with others who have recovered from paralysis and their families.

Three self-help stroke clubs, whose members have had strokes, exist in New Brunswick. The clubs can be reached as follows:

- Fredericton Stroke Club, c/o Donna LeBlanc, University of New Brunswick Faculty of Nursing, Fredericton, N.B. E3B 5A3
- Saint John Stroke Club, c/o Evelyn Waters, P.O. Box 3914, Station B, Saint John, N.B. E2M 5E6
- Moncton Stroke Club, c/o Doris Dealey, 248 Buckingham Avenue, Riverview, N.B. E1B 2N8

Relief Care

Caregivers and others in the family who need a break

can obtain assistance from the government-run Relief Care Program. So long as the care receiver meets the program's assessment criteria, he or she will be admitted for a period of between 7 and 30 days at a participating nursing home. Caregivers may avail themselves of this service no more than once every six months.

For more information, contact your local Public Health Services office.

Help with Vehicle Modification

If you and/or the elderly person you care for need to modify a vehicle so that she or he can use it, as either driver or passenger, help is available under the provincial transportation department's Vehicle Retrofitting Program. So long as the elder meets the program's criteria, a grant will be made.

For more information, contact the Department of Transportation, P.O. Box 6000, Fredericton, New Brunswick E3B 5H1.

Learning in Later Life

All four universities in the province—Mount Allison University, St. Thomas University, l'Université de Moncton, and the University of New Brunswick—welcome older students into credit courses, and all but Mount Allison also admit them into non-credit courses.

For those aged 60 or older, UNB, Mount Allison, and St. Thomas waive tuition fees for credit courses.

At the Université de Moncton, the qualifying age is 65 or older.

If elderly students cannot travel to a university campus, UNB and the Université de Moncton both offer education at a distance. UNB has audio-taped courses, audio-teleconferencing, and home study options, and the Université de Moncton has televised courses.

For more information, contact the university of your choice at these addresses:

- Mount Allison University, Sackville, N.B. E0A 3C0
- St. Thomas University, P.O. Box 4569, Fredericton, N.B. E3B 5G3
- Université de Moncton, Moncton Campus, Moncton, N.B. E1A 3E9
- Université de Moncton, Edmundston Campus, Centre Universitaire St. Louis Maillet, Edmundston, N.B. E3V 2S8
- Université de Moncton, Shippagan Campus, Centre Universitaire de Shippagan, Shippagan, N.B. E0B 2P0
- University of New Brunswick, Fredericton Campus, P.O. Box 4400, Fredericton, N.B. E3B 5A3
- University of New Brunswick, Saint John Campus, P.O. Box 5050, Saint John, N.B. E2L 4L5

Third Age Wellness

The Université du Troisième Age has as its goal the promotion of a healthful lifestyle for the elderly, mostly through physical activity programs. Activities include walking, aquatics, and skiing, and are held throughout the year, usually on a once-a-week basis. Weekend workshops are also offered at the Université de Moncton and the Memramcook Institute. Participants pay a fee of $15. The organization serves the southeastern region of the province and operates in the French language only.

For more information, contact Université du Troisième Age, Jacqueline Bouchard Building, Local 172, Université de Moncton, Moncton, New Brunswick E1A 3E9.

Newfoundland

Activities Galore Centre

The Seniors Resource Centre in St. John's offers perhaps the widest variety of programs and services provided at one location.

Here is just a sampling. A referral line can be used to find all the services and resources available in the community. A volunteer driving program provides elders with transportation to programs at the centre itself and elsewhere. A volunteer visiting service reaches out to elders living alone in the community. Members of a mall walkers' club head out for their walk once a week and receive discounts at participating stores in the mall. Victorian Order of Nurses personnel come in to staff foot-care clinics. Snowbusters is a program which matches elders with young volunteers who will clear snow so that the elders can walk out onto the street. Free income tax clinics are held.

For more information, contact the Seniors Resource Centre, Prince Charles Building, 120 Torbay Road, Suite 104, St. John's, Newfoundland A1A 2G8.

Aid for Those with Alzheimer's

The Wandering Patient Registry has two goals. One is to ensure the police have at hand all the information they need when searching for or identifying someone who is lost or wandering due to Alzheimer's or another form of dementia. The other is to reduce the risks for those who are lost and the anxiety of caregivers.

Caregivers and others who want to register those at risk of wandering should contact the Alzheimer Society for an appointment. One of the society's staff will register the wanderer. This service is entirely voluntary, and users pay no fees. Information registered includes details of the appearance and characteristic behaviours of the wanderer. It is entered into a computer and is readily available to police officers in the region.

For more information, contact the Alzheimer Society Resource Centre, c/o L.A. Miller Centre, 100 Forest Road, St. John's, Newfoundland A1A 1E5.

Drivers' Refresher Course

A refresher course whose aim is to improve older people's driving skills and to help them keep their driving licences and to drive safely is called 55 Alive, 55 being the entry age.

Instructors are trained by the Canada Safety Council. The course consists of six sessions. Participants learn about the characteristics of mature drivers and physical changes that may affect their performance. In two of the sessions, they go over the mechanics of driving and interacting with other traffic. A session on accident prevention, bad driving conditions due to weather, and other road users is followed by a final session which reviews the course content and promotes discussion of it.

For more information, contact the Newfoundland Safety Council, 93 Water Street, St. John's, Newfoundland A1C 5V5.

The "No Books" Library

An innovative and highly useful service is known as the "No Books" library. In fact, it is a collection of various assistive aids and devices such as those detailed in Chapter 7 of this book, divided into five categories: communication, hygiene, dressing, eating, and homemaking. Its purpose is to acquaint elders with these aids to enable them to decide which, if any, would make living independently easier for them.

Users of the "No Books" library may try out aids on the spot. (There is a kitchen, where cooking aids may be tried out.) Or they may sign them out for two weeks and try them out at home. The library also advises patrons where the aids can be bought and what they cost.

For more information, contact the library at Civic #4, Independent Living Centre, 4 Escasoni Place, St. John's, Newfoundland A1A 3R6.

Nova Scotia

Eye Care in the Home

For elders in their own homes or in retirement complexes or hospitals who have difficulty getting to an optician, Senior Optical Services of Bedford will send licensed opticians out at no extra charge. The service includes 10 to 20 per cent price reductions and a one-year guarantee on all eyeglass parts and accessories. If the client needs an eye examination, the service will also provide transportation.

For more information, contact Senior Optical Services at P.O. Box 652, Bedford, Nova Scotia B4A 3H4.

Self-Help Stroke Club

As noted above (see page 147), those who have experienced a stroke and their immediate families derive great benefit from contact with others in the same situation.

The Halifax Stroke Club operates in the same way as those in New Brunswick. For more information, write to Mrs. Anna Redmond, 10 Burns Drive, Halifax, Nova Scotia B3P 1V5.

Ontario

Free Legal Aid for the Needy

The Advocacy Centre for the Elderly (ACE) is a legal aid clinic for elderly people who have low incomes. Its services are free; its costs are paid by the Ontario Legal Aid Plan. ACE typically helps clients who have problems with pensions or other benefits; those who are in disagreement with children or other family members who believe they are mentally incompetent; those who are not happy with the care they are receiving in an institution; those who are being abused physically, verbally, or financially; those being discriminated against on the basis of age; and many others.

Advice is often given over the telephone. If face-to-face conversation is necessary, the elder can make an appointment to go to the ACE office. Or if he or she is unable to come to the office for medical reasons, an ACE staff member will come to the home or institution.

For more information, write ACE at Suite 902, Eglinton Avenue East, Toronto, Ontario M4P 1E2.

Welcome House

Older people newly arrived in Canada may find the help they need at the Ministry of Citizenship's Ontario Welcome Houses. There, staff can provide counsel about government grants and special programs for elders, and information about clubs for older people, nursing homes, and low-income housing. As well, staff will also help people fill out forms and applications if required, and will also refer inquirers to appropriate cultural groups. Welcome House services, which are free of charge, are offered in 39 languages and dialects.

For more information, contact the Ontario Welcome House nearest to you. Houses are located at:

- 2 King Street West, Hamilton, Ont. L8P 1A1
- Confederation Place, 90 Dundas Street West, Mississauga, Ont. L5B 2T5
- Downsview Plaza, 1056A Wilson Avenue, Downsview, Ont. M3K 1G6
- Brimley Place, 4439 Sheppard Avenue East, Scarborough, Ont. M1S 1V3
- 132 St. Patrick Street, Toronto, Ont. M5T 1V1

Help for Those with Diabetes

Three Toronto hospitals—Toronto General, Women's College, and Mount Sinai—have banded together to form Tridec, a program that teaches people with diabetes how to manage and control their problem. Courses—three days for those using pills or controlling their diabetes with diet and exercise, four days for those who use needles—are given by dietitians and nurses. As well, medical practitioners may take part, talking about the latest research findings concerning diabetes. Those taking the course pay nothing; the cost of the course is borne by the provincial health care plan.

If you think an elder in your care could benefit from taking a Tridec course, discuss it with her or him, then one or both of you should talk about it to the family physician, since patients taking the course must be referred by a medical practitioner.

Note that other hospitals may run educational courses for people with diabetes. Check by calling hospitals in your area.

Stroke Associations

The Stroke Recovery Association of Ontario has 35 chapters throughout the province. Members are those who have had strokes and their spouses or other family members. The aim of the chapters is to foster recovery in speech, movement of limbs, and general health.

For more information and/or to find a chapter near you, contact the association at 585 Trethewey Drive, Toronto, Ontario M6M 4B8.

Info Centre

The Centre for People with Disabilities is on the premises of the Metropolitan Toronto Reference Library, at 789 Yonge Street. You will find there information on disabilities and services for those who have disabilities, large-print newspapers and magazines, talking books and recorded magazines. The centre also has specialized equipment for those with vision impairment, such as magnifiers, Visualtek (a type of closed-circuit television which enlarges print up to 60 times), a braille typewriter, TDD (hooked up to a telephone, it permits the user to type out a message instead of speaking, and to receive a typed reply), and a Kurzwell Personal Reader (a computerized device which scans the printed word, then reads it in a synthetic voice).

Info Phone

If you live in the Toronto area, and if you and/or an elder you care for want information on general health topics, you may find what you are seeking by dialing 972–7500. This will connect you to the Doctors Hospital Health Phone, an around-the-clock service which permits those with touch-tone telephones to listen to taped messages on a number of topics, among them heart and stroke, nutrition, mental health, alcohol and drug abuse, and schizophrenia.

The service is multilingual: callers can receive the messages in English, French, Italian, Portuguese, Spanish, or Chinese.

Note that some other hospitals in Ontario and elsewhere in Canada offer a similar service. Check with hospitals in your area.

Suitably Attired

Traditions: Senior Clothing Designs Ltd. custom-makes garments for older women. Among its designs are dresses to fit and conceal larger waistlines, and garments that fit the curved backs of clients with osteoporosis. If so desired, it will fill special orders, such as using Velcro closures and adding buttons purely for show. Traditions' storefront is at 1177 Yonge Street, Toronto, Ontario M4T 1W2. The company also runs a mail-order service, keeping clients' measurements on file in case new orders are received. Those outside the Toronto area may ask for a catalogue to be sent or order garments by dialing toll-free 1–800–567–1177.

Prince Edward Island

Activity Centre

The Seniors Active Living Centre came into being in Charlottetown thanks to a movement spearheaded by the Prince Edward Island Senior Citizens' Federation. It is open on weekdays (but can also open on weekends for special events). Close to 20 programs are offered: they include t'ai chi, bowling, hearing clinics, defensive driving courses, advocacy, flower arranging, and crafts. Speakers often come in to talk on topics such as gardening, financial planning, and travel. Those attending enjoy low-cost lunches and special-event teas, as well as special-event entertainment and activities.

For more information, contact the P.E.I. Senior Citizens' Federation at P.O. Box 152, Charlottetown, Prince Edward Island C1A 7K4.

Dietary Smarts Course

If you and/or the elder you look after want to know how to choose and prepare foods that promote cardiovascular fitness, the Foods Course/Grocery Store Tour may be for you.

For more information, contact the Education Director, Heart and Stroke Foundation of P.E.I., 40 Queen Street, Charlottetown, Prince Edward Island C1A 7K4.

Fashions for Elders

Island Comfort Clothing makes fashionable, reasonably priced clothing for older people. Dresses are made of easy-care, washable fabrics, armholes are spacious, and buttons and zippers are placed where they are easy to manage. The company also makes open-back clothing with Velcro fasteners for elders who cannot stand up or raise their arms. The operator, Aletha Smith, will set up a store in a nursing home. She also has a store in her home or will deliver clothes to customers' homes. The business is also mail order: spring/summer and fall/winter catalogues are published.

For more information, contact Island Comfort Clothing, 318 Lower Malpeque Road, Charlottetown, Prince Edward Island C1E 1S8.

Home Eye Care

For those who are housebound, Vogue Optical will send

personnel to the home to fit, repair, or adjust glasses. Eye examinations can also be arranged.

For more information, contact Vogue Optical, 5 Brackley Point Road, Charlottetown, Prince Edward Island C1A 6X8.

Quebec

Legal Counsel

In Montreal, call the Legal Phone for advice and information on why and how to make a will, inheritance procedures, and the duties of a will's executor(s). The number to call is (514) 845–0888.

If you need the name of a lawyer or notary, contact the information service of the Barreau de Montréal at 866–2490 or the Chambre des notaires at 879–1793. Staff will give you the name of a lawyer or notary, and you will receive an initial 30-minute consultation at reduced rates.

Help by Phone for Substance Abusers

Quebeckers who need information about alcohol and other drugs and about programs and services for substance abusers can dial a toll-free number and receive the information in either French or English. The service is administered by the Information and Referral Centre of Greater Montreal and operates around the clock, seven days a week. Trained volunteers overseen by qualified professionals take the calls and provide the information.

Callers in the immediate Montreal area should dial 527–2626. Those in all other areas of Quebec should dial 1–800–265–2626.

Help for People Who Have Had Strokes

Those who have had strokes could benefit greatly from joining the Jewish General Hospital Stroke Club in Montreal. Members do speech stimulation and other exercises, play games, go on outings, listen to speakers, and enjoy arts and crafts. They meet once a week in the morning and remain on the premises until after luncheon.

For more information, contact the club at Temple Emanu-El Beth Shalom, 395 Elm Street, Westmount, Quebec H3Z 1Z4.

Care for Caregivers

Jewish Support Services for the Elderly (JSSE) in Montreal organizes support groups for spouses and mature children who are caring for elders. Those who join a "Care for the Caregiver" group meet either weekly or every other week to share information, help each other solve problems, and generally provide peer support. Often, an expert on some aspect of eldercare will talk to the group.

For more information, contact JSSE at 5151 Côte

Ste-Catherine, Suite 300, Montreal, Quebec H3W 1M6.

Elders Helping Elders

Job Aid is a Golden Age Association program which arranges both full- and part-time employment for older people by older people. Among those hired are nurses' aides, home helpers, handymen, and companions.

For more information, write to the Golden Age Association, Job Aid, 5700 Westbury, Room 206, Montreal, Quebec H3W 3E8.

Saskatchewan

Transportation Help for Those with Disabilities

The Saskatchewan Transportation Company has specially designed chairs for travellers who are wheelchair-bound and who are travelling either to or from Estevan, Melfort, Melville, North Battleford, Prince Albert, Regina, Saskatoon, Swift Current, Weyburn, and Yorkton.

As well, a traveller who is deemed unable to travel alone by the Canadian Rehabilitation Council for the Disabled or one of its affiliated members, and who is accompanied by an adult assistant, pays one fare only.

For more information, contact the Saskatchewan Transportation Company, 2041 Hamilton Street, Regina, Saskatchewan S4P 2E2.

WISE Clinics

WISE is an acronym for Well Information Services for the Elderly, a program which came into being in Saskatchewan in 1982, and now has offshoots across the province, and which deserves to be copied right across Canada. If prevention is better than cure, then here is prevention *par excellence.*

WISE Wellness Clinics are set up, with the assistance of health care professionals, under the aegis of social and other clubs for seniors or seniors' residences. Members of the club receive regular health checks and counsel. Procedures may include any or all of the following: hypertension testing, urine testing, vision and hearing testing, haemoglobin testing, blood sugar testing, health, medication and nutrition counselling, and minor foot care.

There are more than 100 WISE Wellness Clinics in the province—too large a number to be identified here. So if you want to know if there is a clinic near you, or if you want more information, contact WISE at 23 Bell Crescent, Saskatoon, Saskatchewan S7J 2W2. If you belong to a club or live in a home that could benefit from having a clinic, ask for a copy of the WISE *Wellness Clinic Manual: A Guide to Start a* WISE *Wellness Clinic.*

Respite for Caregivers

Caregivers can enjoy some well-earned relief and respite by using one of two programs organized by the Community Living Division of Saskatchewan Social Services. In one, elders go into one of two community resource homes on a temporary basis. One home is Elmwood Lodge in Saskatoon, the other the Regina Residential Resource Home in Regina. Or, if the elder cannot easily get to either Saskatoon or Regina, an outreach program will provide funding to the caregiver for respite services in the home or the community.

In both cases, the cost of respite care is nominal. And in both cases, caregivers may have up to 60 days a year of respite through these programs.

For more information, contact the Community Living Division, Saskatchewan Social Services, 110 Ominicia Street West, Moose Jaw, Saskatchewan S6H 6Y5, or one of Social Services' branch offices: they are located in Estevan, Humboldt, LaRonge, Melfort, North Battleford, Prince Albert, Regina, Rosetown, Saskatoon, Swift Current, Weyburn, and Yorkton.

Foot Care

Those requiring diagnosis and treatment of foot problems can find what they need at the Saskatchewan Chiropody Program's 10 full-time and 23 part-time clinics.

Patients must be referred to the program by a family physician, home care nursing coordinator, public health nurse, VON worker, or director of care at a retirement or nursing home. Patients pay a visit participation fee and, if any special orthotics are needed, they pay for these too.

For more information, contact your regional health office or Saskatchewan Health, 3475 Albert Street, Regina, Saskatchewan S4S 6X6.

Free Legal Aid

Those aged 65 or older who receive the federal Guaranteed Income Supplement (paid to those who have low incomes), and need legal help, can receive assistance at no cost. The Law Society of Saskatchewan has a referral program, matching those who need legal aid but can't afford it with lawyers willing to provide that aid without charge.

The only cost to clients is reimbursement of any out-of-pocket expenses the lawyer may incur. How much these might amount to and how the client will provide reimbursement should be discussed at the first meeting.

For more information, call the Saskatchewan Lawyer Referral Service at 359–1767 if you live within local calling distance of Regina, or at 1–800–667–9886 if calling from elsewhere in the province.

Yukon

Help for Those with Speech and Hearing Problems

Anyone suffering from aphasia, a speech disorder that can result from a stroke or a blow to the head, can receive help from the territorial government's Speech/ Language Pathology program. Likewise, anyone with impaired hearing can receive help from the same program. An audiologist will conduct hearing tests, assist the client in selecting a hearing aid, and generally offer advice on how to cope with impaired hearing.

Patients with aphasia need no referral, but those with hearing loss need a referral from a family physician, public health nurse, or social worker.

For more information, contact Speech and Hearing Services, 2nd Floor, Royal Bank Building, 4114 4th Avenue, Suite 202, Whitehorse, Yukon Y1A 4N7.

Coping with Loss and Grief

Those who are terminally ill and their caregivers can receive help from the Hospice Yukon Society, which disseminates information about dying, loss, and grief. Those who are terminally ill and those suffering grief after a death are helped and supported by specially trained volunteers. Courses of support for groups of bereaved people are held periodically. The society also has a resource library of books, pamphlets, and audiovisual materials, and will mail items to clients living outside Whitehorse.

For more information, contact the Volunteer Coordinator, Hospice Yukon Society, 211 Elliott Street, Whitehorse, Yukon Y1A 2A2.

Multiple Resource Centre

Numerous free services are provided at the Seniors Information Centre in Whitehorse. Users can receive information and, where relevant, application forms, concerning health, recreation and education, income tax, pensions, Letter Carrier Alert programs, lending libraries, and housing.

For more information, contact Seniors Information Centre, 106 Main Street, Suite 3, Whitehorse, Yukon Y1A 2A8.

CHAPTER ELEVEN
ELDERS ON THE MOVE

THE FACTS THAT OUR KNOWLEDGE ABOUT THE PHYSIOLOGY and psychology of aging is increasing, and that more and more people are taking good care of themselves and hence remaining in great shape in later life, have had many effects on our society, not the least of which is the growth in the number of older travellers. They may have taken early retirement, are probably relatively wealthy, and are keen to be out there, on the move and seeing other parts of the world.

And the world of travel and touring is being tailored to attract them and to meet their needs. All manner of discounts, and even freebies, are being offered, and travel agencies that cater exclusively or largely to older people are springing up. As well, facilities exist that ensure that no one with any type of physical disability is barred from travelling or joining tours.

How old is the "older" traveller? Generally, ask whether any concessions are granted to those 55 and older. (I once heard of a Texas organization for whom "senior" meant 45 and older, but that was surely an aberration.)

As well as the sources listed below, you'll almost certainly find advertisements and articles about tours and other arrangements for older travellers in many of the general-interest magazines and newspapers listed in Chapter 13.

PREPARATION IS KEY

Before getting down to the details of various travel and tour organizations and arrangements of interest to older people, let's take a quick look at what documents older travellers—or any travellers, for that matter—should take along with them. Here's a list of the most critical items.

- Personal identification of some kind, probably a passport and/or a driving licence.
- Any provincial health care card and/or other health insurance documentation.
- Information about any insurance you may have, including travel insurance.
- The name and telephone number of your family physician.
- A summary of your recent medical history, including information about any conditions or disabilities you currently have.
- A list of the medications, both prescription and over-the-counter, you currently take.

- If you take drugs, a letter from your family physician confirming this, to satisfy customs officials that you have good reason to have drugs—and possibly syringes—in your luggage.
- The name and telephone number of the person or persons you would want to have contacted if you were to fall ill, have an accident, or be otherwise involved in an emergency situation.

Gathering together the necessary information and documentation is but one step in preparing to travel. Some other important pre-trip activities are described below.

Get into good shape before you light out. If you already exercise regularly, increase the level of exercise weeks, or even months, before a long trip. Maintain that level while you are away. If you don't exercise regularly, now is the time to start.

Consult with your family physician, advising which country or countries you will be visiting, to make sure you have the requisite immunizations. Also check to see whether any of your medications need to be changed. For instance, some diuretics and some antibiotics make those who take them more sensitive to the sun.

Make sure you have adequate travel and accident insurance. (More information on the former is provided later in this chapter.)

THE BENEFITS OF IAMAT

Among key preparations, consider joining the International Association for Medical Assistance to Travellers (IAMAT). The association, which is in touch with a worldwide network of physicians, accepts all who wish to join, at no charge; however, members may make voluntary, tax-deductible contributions (and will derive extra benefits if their contributions are above a certain level). Members receive the following:

- A directory of physicians in 125 countries whose professional qualifications have been reviewed and approved, who received medical training in either North America or Europe, and who speak English.
- A clinical record to be completed by you and your family physician, which you give to an IAMAT physician treating you, so he or she will be fully apprised of the state of your health.
- A world immunization chart, showing the protection required by governments, and that recommended over and above the governmental requirement.
- A world chart showing where you will be at risk of contracting malaria and what protection you should take.
- A world chart showing where you will be at risk of contracting schistosomiasis, a severe endemic disease which is quite prevalent in hot climates, and what steps you should take to avoid becoming infected.

The physicians listed in the directory have agreed that

member travellers may call upon them. They have also agreed to a reasonable fee schedule.

IAMAT's head office is at 40 Regal Road, Guelph, Ontario N1K 1B5.

TRAVEL GOODIES CLOSE AT HAND

Many older travellers have already visited the more common and popular destinations, and specifically want to go on tours to or travel independently in more off-the-beaten-track regions—South America, perhaps, or Australasia, or island destinations in southeast Asia.

However, don't overlook bargains closer to home, perhaps for shorter trips or even weekend jaunts.

For instance, many provinces have reduced rates for fishing and/or hunting licences for older people, and discounted or free camping in provincial parks. Check with your provincial tourism department or the tourism department of provinces you and/or your elder will be travelling in.

At the same time, ask provincial tourism departments if there are any other concessions for older visitors. You may find you can receive discounts at certain tourist sites and/or museums. For instance, in British Columbia, Barkerville Historic Town, Fort Steele Heritage Town, and the Royal British Columbia Museum in Victoria all give 50 per cent discounts to older visitors.

As well, the B.C. Ferry Corporation allows the elderly to travel free of charge Mondays to Thursdays (with the exception of statutory holidays) year round. The exceptions are ferries serving the Inside Passage and Queen Charlotte Island routes; on these routes, rates are discounted 33 per cent for the elderly seven days a week.

In eastern Canada, older customers get breaks at ski resorts. Rates for them are reduced—in one case, waived entirely—in Ontario at Blue Mountain near Collingwood and Horseshoe near Barrie, and in Quebec at Gray Rocks in the Laurentians and Mount Orford in the Eastern Townships.

INTERGENERATIONAL TRAVEL

Travelling together is a great way for grandparents and their grandchildren to get to know each other really well or to make existing good relationships even better. Retired people have the time to go with the kids on longer trips during school vacations, a luxury parents with limited vacation time may not have.

Grandtravel is one of several organizations marketing intergenerational travel packages. It has some really off-the-beaten-track products: how about learning how to build an igloo during an Alaskan wilderness adventure, or tracking wild animals on a Kenya safari adventure?

For more information about Grandtravel, write The Ticket Counter, 6900 Wisconsin Avenue, Suite 706, Chevy Chase, Maryland, U.S.A. 20815, or call, toll-free, 1-800-247-7651.

Three British Columbian hotels—the Hotel Vancouver and the Waterfront Centre Hotel, both in Vancouver, and the Empress Hotel in Victoria—offer what they call the "nannies and grannies package," with reduced prices for grandparents and children travelling together. For more details, call, toll-free, 1-800-268-9411.

In Quebec, Camp B'nai Brith in the Laurentians runs an intergenerational camping program with young campers alongside those aged 60 or older.

For more details, contact B'nai Brith at 5151 Côte Ste. Catherine, Suite 205, Montreal, Quebec H3W 1M6.

FOREVER YOUNG

Forever Young is the name of a program offered at six Club Med villages in the sunny south. It allows members aged 60 or older to spend one week at the village of their choice for $150 less than the regular rate.

The villages, chosen because they have great golf courses, and excellent shopping and nightlife nearby, are Eleuthera and Paradise Island in the Bahamas, Sandpiper in Florida, Caravelle in Guadeloupe, and Cancún and Ixtapa in Mexico.

At Eleuthera, Ixtapa, and Sandpiper, a Kids Free program runs in the summer, offering another opportunity to enjoy an inexpensive intergenerational vacation.

For more information, contact Club Med at 162 Cumberland Street, Toronto, Ontario M5R 1A8, or dial toll-free 1-800-363-6033, if calling from Quebec or Atlantic Canada, and 1-800-268-1160, if calling from Ontario or any province west of Ontario.

ADVENTURE KNOWS NO AGE BARRIER

Fully escorted adventure tours for groups of people aged 55 or older is the specialty of ElderTreks. Destinations include Costa Rica, Sarawak, Sabah, Vietnam, Ecuador, Thailand, Indonesia, and Borneo. At time of writing, tours in Belize and possibly Australia were also in the works.

Those taking part in a tour should be reasonably fit and able to spend a day walking in a tropical climate. On every tour there is an adventure side trip; for instance, on a tour in Thailand, participants spend three days and two nights hiking between and staying in tribal villages, and also riding elephants. Participants in these side trips must produce a medical questionnaire completed by their family physicians.

For more information, contact your regular travel agent or ElderTreks, Passages Expeditions, 597 Markham Street, Toronto, Ontario M6G 2L7.

WORDS OF WISDOM

Handi-Travel: A Resource Book for Disabled and Elderly Travellers, by Cinnie Noble, is a first-rate publication containing a wealth of information on all manner of topics, from air, rail, and ship travel to tour packages and accommodations. It is full of little-known facts: for example, many hotel chains (among them Hilton, Holiday Inn, Marriott, Ramada, Sheraton, and Westin), have special rooms, called wheelchair, paraplegic, ambulatory, or handicapped rooms, with features such as raised sinks and vanity tops that accommodate a wheelchair underneath, handrails beside the toilet and in the bath to help those who use walking aids or have balance problems, and ample wheelchair turning space and a telephone in the bathroom.

The book is published by the Canadian Rehabilitation Council for the Disabled (CRCD) in conjunction with the Canadian Transport Commission and Transport Canada: The Transportation Development Centre and the Directorate of Transportation of the Handicapped. It is available from the CRCD, at 45 Sheppard Avenue East, Suite 801, Toronto, Ontario M2N 5W9.

The Intrepid Traveller is a highly readable magazine full of information and tips for older travellers, edited by veteran travel writers Carolyn Walton and Susan Hallett. It is published six times a year.

For more information, write The Intrepid Traveller, RR#2, Jasper, Ontario K0G 1G0.

Unbelievably Good Deals and Great Adventures That You Absolutely Can't Get Unless You're Over 50, written by Joan Rattner Heilman, is published in Canada by Fitzhenry & Whiteside Ltd. Content is more American than Canadian, but a new edition is published each year and the author is gradually increasing the Canadian content. The latest (1993) edition is in bookstores now.

The Travellers Medical Services Directory, edited by Milan Korcok and published by James McCartney (both of whom are Canadians), is a mine of information on travel health insurance. It details coverage travellers have under their provincial health plans and qualifications required; provides advice on how to choose a private insurer; and gives information on admission policies for Canadians, acceptance or otherwise of credit cards, and other topics, for 200 hospitals in Arizona and Florida.

At the time of writing, the directory was available at W.H. Smith bookstores and was about to be carried by Shoppers Drug Mart.

WALKING TO WELLNESS

Along with swimming, walking ranks high as a great type of exercise for older people. What better vacation pastime, then, than a walking tour?

A U.S. tour operator, Country Walkers, organizes walking tours in a number of countries, among them Switzerland, England, the United States, New Zealand, and France. Those taking part choose from among the tours listed in a 16-page catalogue and, once they have made reservations, receive a list of clothing and other items they will need to take on the tour and a list of suggested readings for those who like to bone up on an area in advance. On the tour, they walk anywhere from four to ten miles per day.

To receive a catalogue, write Country Walkers, P.O. Box 180, Waterbury, Vermont, U.S.A. 06576-0180.

Britain, with its wide variety of scenery packaged into a small space, is a great place for walking. The British Tourist Authority has a number of brochures on walking tours in the British Isles. It also has a fold-out map, *Walking in Britain*, which details nearly 60 great walks, and lists companies that conduct them, tourist attractions along the way, and tourist accommodations in the area.

To receive brochures and the map, write to the British Tourist Authority at 111 Avenue Road, Suite 450, Toronto, Ontario M5R 3J8, enclosing an International Reply Coupon (available from any Canada Post outlet) to defray postage costs.

PAIRING UP FOR SAVINGS

Elderly travellers who are widowed, or whose mates just

don't want to travel, will probably want to receive *Connecting: News for Solo Travellers*, a newsletter which features news, advice, and free advertisements from single travellers who want travel companions, either just to have company or to pair up with and hence save on accommodation costs. The newsletter is published six times a year. The company also runs a club for single travellers: members receive a copy of a directory which lists companies that charge lower single supplements, and which reveals other ways to avoid paying the supplement.

For more information, write to Connecting at P.O. Box 29088, Delamont Postal Outlet, 1996 West Broadway, Vancouver, British Columbia V6J 5C2.

The Travel 24 Single Traveller's Club has the same objective—to pair up single travellers. Its parent company, Travel 24 Inc., arranges tours to various parts of the world, and members of the club may come from any part of Canada: perhaps someone from Montreal heading out on a Pacific tour will be paired with someone who joins the group in Vancouver. It also arranges tours or cruises on which no single supplement is payable by those not sharing accommodation.

For more information, write to Travel 24 Inc. at 1575 Steeles Avenue East, Suite 109, Willowdale, Ontario M2M 3Y8.

The Selective Singles Travel Registry provides members with a brochure listing other members and their characteristics, so that they can do their own pairing. Members supply information in a number of categories, including age, whether they are interested in all-male or all-female groups, the number of trips they take each year and the amount they spend, whether or not they are smokers, and what kind of recreational activities and sports they enjoy.

For more information, write to Selective Singles Travel Registry at 2245 Dunwin Drive, Mississauga, Ontario L5L 1A3.

TravelShare is a club for women travellers. Its members meet regularly and socialize, as well as teaming up for travel. Sometimes they travel in pairs and sometimes in groups. Many members are keen travellers whose husbands can't or simply don't want to accompany them. The club's newsletter carries information about forthcoming trips and publishes lists of members in need of travel companions.

For more information, write TravelShare, 44 Victoria Street, Suite 1315, Toronto, Ontario M5C 1Y5.

SPECIFICALLY SERVING ELDERS

Quite a number of travel agencies and other organizations specifically tailor products to the needs of older travellers and may or may not provide discounts. Here is just a small sampling.

The following travel agents in the Halifax-Dartmouth area all provide discounts for elders' groups:

Nova Tours, 60604 Quinpool Road, Halifax, Nova Scotia B3L 1A1; Atlantic Tours Ltd., P.O. Box 3596, Halifax, Nova Scotia B3J 3J2, toll-free telephone 1-800-565-7173; Airport Transfer Co. Ltd., Nova Charter Services, 71 Simmonds Drive, Dartmouth, Nova Scotia B3B 1N7; Harvey's Travel, 1796 Granville Street, Halifax, Nova Scotia B3J 1X7.

Senior Citizens Tour and Travel Inc. arranges all-inclusive tours for travellers aged 50 or older. Tours may be leisurely stay-put ones, or safaris and other more adventurous junkets. The company receives inquiries from many parts of the country, and, when asked to do so, will try to match up single travellers with others so they will not have to pay the single supplement. The original office is in Toronto; by the time you read this, offices will almost certainly be open in Hamilton and London, Ontario, as well.

For more information, contact the company at 225 Eglinton Avenue West, Toronto, Ontario M4R 1A9. Callers in Ontario and Quebec may dial, toll-free, 1-800-268-3492.

Seniors Carefree Travel Inc. also caters to those aged 50 or older. It operates individual and group tours which range all the way from a one-day junket to Niagara Falls to a month in China. Its package prices almost always include insurance, transportation to and from airports, and gratuities. For insurance reasons, it cannot accommodate clients in wheelchairs.

For more information write the company at 4528A Kingston Road, Suite 4, West Hill, Ontario M1E 2N8.

In Manitoba, these elders' organizations provide travel services: Age and Opportunity Travel, 304-323 Portage Avenue, Winnipeg, Manitoba R3B 2C1; MSOS Travel Services, 803-294 Portage Avenue, Winnipeg, Manitoba R3C 0B9; Lions Manor Travel Services, 320 Sherbrook Street, Winnipeg, Manitoba R3B 2W6.

ACCESS FOR ALL

The Accessible Transportation Policy and Programs of Transport Canada has provided many hundreds of thousands of dollars to those in the tourism and travel business one way or another to ensure that those with disabilities are able to travel freely. All the following services have received some funding from Transport Canada.

Both Budget Rent a Car and Thrifty Car Rental have hand control–operated automobiles and wheelchair-accessible vans for rent at major airports in Canada. For information and reservations with Budget, dial 1–800–268–8900. For information and reservations with Thrifty, dial 1–800–367–2277.

Park 'n Fly in Vancouver and Toronto has wheelchair-accessible shuttle buses. The shuttle service is free and runs every 5 to 10 minutes.

Penetang-Midland Coach Line has wheelchair-accessible buses running on its free service between Terminals 1, 2, and 3 at Lester B. Pearson International Airport in Toronto.

Time Air and Air BC, both of which operate small aircraft and provide connections with Air Canada and Canadian Airlines International, have accessible boarding lifts that can be used by all passengers, including those with disabilities and those in wheelchairs. The lifts are at the airports in Toronto, Vancouver, and Victoria.

Air Nova has an accessible boarding lift at Halifax airport and, by the time you read this, will almost certainly have accessible lifts at the airports in Sydney, Nova Scotia, and Charlottetown, Prince Edward Island, as well.

SPECIAL CARE + HOLIDAYS

Horizon Holidays, a long-standing leader in organizing luxury escorted tours, goes to the front of the pack again with a highly innovative arrangement and a first in Canada. This is "Special Care +," a new division of the company whose tour offerings will make it possible for people with certain medical problems to travel safely and comfortably.

Its first venture off the ground was a Caribbean cruise for those with respiratory problems who are oxygen-dependant. Air Canada provided oxygen for the travellers on the round-trip flight to Miami, and oxygen supplier Medigas provided oxygen for them on board ship.

Travelling with the group was a physician specializing in respiratory ailments, a registered respiratory therapist, and an intensive care nurse.

At the time of writing, more tours for those with respiratory problems were in the works, specifically another Caribbean cruise, a cruise up the west coast from Vancouver as far as Glacier Bay in Alaska, and a nine-day Bermuda vacation. Horizon is also considering expanding its Special Care + offerings, with tours designed for people who have other medical problems.

For more information, contact Horizon Holidays at 160 John Street, Toronto, Ontario M5V 2X8.

BREATHE EASY

Those with respiratory problems causing them to need supplemental oxygen may also breathe easy while travelling with VIA Rail and most major airlines, including Air Canada.

Airlines require at least 72 hours' and preferably one week's notice of the disabled person's intention to travel. They require that this notice be provided by the traveller's family physician. They provide portable oxygen units and charge a fee for doing so.

VIA Rail requires two to three days' notice of intent to travel. Travellers with VIA use their own oxygen supply and give VIA personnel information about the type they use.

For more information, contact your travel agent or local airline and VIA Rail offices.

SEPTEMBER SAVINGS

Anyone aged 50 or older can reap substantial savings by joining the September Days Club and staying at Days Inns. (At the time of writing, there were more than 30 Days Inns in Canada, the vast majority of them in Ontario, with a few in Alberta, British Columbia, Nova Scotia, and Quebec.)

Those who join the club pay a modest annual fee and in return receive discounts of at least 15 per cent on room rates and 10 per cent on meal costs and gift shop purchases. At some of the chain's out-of-town establishments on highways, discounts may run as high as 40 per cent. Among other benefits, club members receive discounts of up to 50 per cent at participating theme parks and entertainment attractions, free flight insurance on air travel booked through the club, and free club membership for their spouses. They also receive *Golden Years*, a quarterly newsletter.

For more information, write to Days Inn—Canada at 2 St. Clair Avenue West, Suite 700, Toronto, Ontario M4V 1L5, or dial, toll-free, 1-800-325-2525.

BENEFITS FOR RAIL RIDERS

Those who travel by rail have the satisfaction of knowing they are indulging in an environmentally sounder practice than travel by automobile or aircraft. And, as I discovered while travelling coast to coast by rail three years ago, they really get to know a country and enjoy good company along the way.

On top of all that, older people receive substantial discounts when travelling by train.

VIA Rail gives a 10 per cent discount to travellers aged 60 or older. If travellers give five days' notice (in some locations, seven days' notice) of their intention to ride the rails, they will receive a whopping 40 per cent discount.

Amtrak, the U.S. passenger rail service, gives a 15 per cent discount to travellers aged 62 years or older, provided they travel on Monday through Thursday. Those travelling on Fridays, Saturdays, or Sundays do not receive discounts.

Britrail, the British passenger rail service, gives travellers aged 60 or older a 10 per cent discount on passes only, not on individual tickets.

For more information, contact your local travel agent.

FLYING HIGH

Those who are at least 55 years old become "privileged travellers" with British Airways. In return for a fee that is modest compared with the savings that can be had, fliers receive a Privileged Traveller Card. This earns them a 10 per cent discount on airfares from Montreal, Toronto, or Vancouver to anywhere in the United Kingdom, no matter whether they are travelling economy, business, or first class, and a 10 per cent discount on all land arrangements featured in the airline's London-Plus brochure (obtainable from a travel agent), including the cost of hotel accommodation, automobile rental, and theatre tickets. If they must cancel a booking or change it, they do not pay the normal flight-cancellation penalties. They may take along a fellow traveller of any age who will enjoy the same benefits so long as the tickets are bought at the same time and the companion follows the same itinerary. As well, they receive a quarterly newsletter containing information about events in Britain, travel tips, and extra travel discounts.

For more information, contact your travel agent.

BENEFITS FOR JOINERS

Members of the Canadian Association of Retired Persons (an organization you'll learn more about in Chapter 12) can benefit from travel discounts when they hit the road. The association has made arrangements with a number of organizations which have agreed to give discounts to members who either make advance reservations or provide proof of membership when making reservations. Among those giving discounts are Avis

Rent A Car, Comfort Inns, The Cruise Professionals Ltd., Howard Johnson Inns and Hotels, Journey's End Hotels, Suites, and Motels, and Quality Inns.

For more information, write to CARP at 27 Queen Street East, Suite 1304, Toronto, Ontario M5C 2M6.

HELPING TRAVELLERS IN NEED

A mother-and-daughter team has set up an innovative and compassionate organization to help older people with low incomes who want to travel but do not have the means.

Torontonians Shirley and Robin Cannon (mother and daughter, respectively), who own and operate an agency, Seniors Travel World, also run the Seniors Foundation, an organization which will help those who need to travel for emergency reasons, who need a restful holiday to improve their health, or who want to travel to meet up with family members they have not seen for a long time.

Funds to enable the older people to travel come from corporate donations and also from part of the proceeds the Cannons will earn from the sale of their book, *50plus Globetrotting—The World of Senior Adult Travel*. Applications for funding will be evaluated by a board of people from the medical, legal, and travel fields.

For more information, contact the Seniors Foundation at 234 Eglinton Avenue East, Suite 507, Toronto, Ontario M4P 1K5.

SAFETY BRIEFING IN BRAILLE

Both Air Canada and Canadian Airlines International have preflight safety briefing cards in braille available upon request. Ask for them when making reservations.

REST ASSURED: INSURE

The Canadian Snowbird Association came into being in 1992 when some out-of-country medical benefits under provincial health plans were cut back. The association has achieved its goal: to provide low-cost medical insurance for those who spend all or part of the winter in the sunny south.

Members of the association can have 100 per cent coverage of up to $1 million with no deductible and no out-of-pocket expenses since payments are made directly to hospitals providing treatment. They can also receive 24-hour medical emergency assistance and emergency evacuation back to Canada if these are required.

For more information, contact the marketer of the plan, Medipac International Inc., Atria II North, 2235 Sheppard Avenue East, Suite 101, North York, Ontario M2J 5B5. Those outside the Toronto area may dial, toll-free, 1–800–563–5105.

Be aware, too, that financial institutions in tandem with credit card companies have set up and marketed quite competitive plans providing travel medical insurance. Among them are Bank of Montreal/Gold MasterCard, Bank of Nova Scotia/Gold Visa, Canada

Trust/Gold MasterCard, Canadian Imperial Bank of Commerce/Gold Visa, Royal Bank/Gold Visa, Royal Trust/Gold MasterCard, Toronto Dominion Bank/ Gold Visa and Gold Elite Visa.

Fees vary considerably, as do terms and periods of coverage. For more information, contact your financial institutions of choice and do some comparison shopping.

CHAPTER TWELVE
A JOINER BE

MANY ELDERLY PEOPLE ENJOY GETTING TOGETHER WITH their peers for various activities, whether oriented toward recreation, learning, health, socializing, or whatever. Realizing at any age that one can learn new skills, or perhaps improve one's health, is exciting and invigorating.

Some elders enjoy getting together to lobby on behalf of elders as a whole. In so doing, they perform a valuable function. No one, after all, is in a better position than they are to know what kind of improvements in our society would benefit the elderly. And again, realizing they can use the wisdom and knowledge they have accumulated over the years to help reshape society and improve their own lot and that of their peers is an exciting discovery.

Whatever the reason for their existence, organizations and facilities for our elders have an overall value. Those who participate in them remain very much in the world at large and in the community, as they deserve to do.

As with services and programs for older Canadians, organizations they can join have proliferated in recent years. Listing every single seniors' club in the country would call for a separate volume. But this chapter at least will introduce you to most of the larger and/or more important organizations. As well, other sources can alert you to the presence of elders' organizations in the neighbourhood. Your local community information centre probably will have information on the subject. Also consult the Yellow Pages, looking for listings under such headings as "Senior Citizens' Organizations and Centres," "Associations," "Recreational Centres," and "Social Service Organizations." A look in the telephone directory at listings starting with "Seniors," "Elders," "Golden," and "Mature" may also yield results. If you are looking for volunteer activities—many retired older people derive great pleasure from doing volunteer work—look at listings starting with "Volunteer." In some cases, "Volunteer" may be preceded by the name of your centre, region, or county.

Another good source of information on elders' organizations and centres is likely to be the local office of the New Horizons program. As you will recall reading in Chapter 10, this program helps fund activities and facilities of all kinds for older people. Contact the New Horizons regional or sub-office nearest to you: they are located in Alberta (Edmonton), British Columbia (Vancouver), Manitoba (Winnipeg), New Brunswick (Moncton), Newfoundland (St. John's), Nova Scotia (Halifax), Ontario (Kitchener and Toronto), Prince Edward Island (Charlottetown), Quebec (Montreal and Quebec City), and Saskatchewan (Regina).

If you are looking for a social centre for older people, contact the Canadian Institute of Senior Centres, which has a listing of more than 500 establishments across Canada. The institute is located at 2615 Northwood Terrace, Halifax, Nova Scotia B3K 3S5.

If you live in Ontario, contact the Older Adults Centres' Association of Ontario to find a social centre. The association is located at 1220 Sheppard Avenue East, Suite 409A, North York, Ontario M2K 2X1. If you live in Quebec, contact the Quebec Federation of Senior Citizens, whose members are some 1,000 elders' clubs in the province. The federation is located at 4545 Pierre-de-Coubertin Avenue, P.O. Box 1000, Postal Station M, Montreal, Quebec H1V 3R2. If you live in Saskatchewan, contact the Saskatchewan Seniors Association Inc., whose membership comprises some 350 clubs. The association is located at 606 Spadina Crescent West, Saskatoon, Saskatchewan S7K 1P1.

Also be aware that your municipal Parks and Recreation Department is probably a good source of information on activity centres and special activities for older people. Ask whoever answers the telephone to connect you with someone involved with older adult programs or centres.

Now here's a rundown, in alphabetical order, of individual organizations.

Alberta Pensioners' and Senior Citizens' Organization. This organization has small branches in the rural areas of the southern part of the province. Acting as an advocacy group for older rural Albertans, it makes representations on their behalf at the annual meeting of the National Pensioners and Senior Citizens Federation (see below).

For more information, contact the organization at P.O. Box 266, Fort Macleod, Alberta P0L 0Z0.

Association Québécoise de Défense des Droits des Retraités et des Préretraités (AQDR). The goals of the AQDR are to band together the retired and the elderly so that they will participate in the defence of their rights, and to defend the rights of retired people to a guaranteed income, decent lodging, adequate homecare and social and medical services, and transportation. It also promotes research and information concerning the specific needs and rights of retired people, disseminating information by means of conferences and printed material. It has almost 40 local chapters throughout the province of Quebec.

For more information, write to the AQDR at 1850 rue Bercy, Suite 113A, Montreal, Quebec H2K 2V2.

Canadian Association of Retired Persons (CARP). CARP is a national, non-profit, non-political association which exists to promote the interests of older Canadians. Through its newsletter (see Chapter 13 for more information), it provides a national forum for the reporting of activities and projects of clubs and other organizations for the elderly, for comment on matters of interest to older people, and for an exchange of views and information. The association also voices the concerns of older Canadians and supports legislative programs that enhance and safeguard their rights to social security and adequate health care and pension incomes.

Those who join CARP derive many benefits from their membership, among them savings in health care and discounts on many products and services, including insurance (both automobile and household), eyeglasses, hotel and motel accommodation, and automobile rentals. Members must be at least 50 years of age and, despite the association's name, they need not be retired.

For more information, write to CARP at 27 Queen Street East, Suite 1304, Toronto, Ontario M5C 2M6.

Canadian Council of Retirees, Ontario Section. The CCR is an organization of retired union members and their spouses in Ontario. Its objectives are to create a centre of thought and action on economic, social, civic, and legislative matters, to petition all levels of government to enact legislation to better the conditions of retired people's health and welfare, and to safeguard the rights of all retirees to a decent standard of living.

At time of writing, the CCR is an Ontario-only organization, but future plans call for its transformation into a national one.

For more information, write to the CCR at 15 Gervais Drive, Room 305, Don Mills, Ontario M3C 1Y8.

Canadian Grey Panthers. This relatively new and growing organization is an intergenerational one (it was founded by a 26-year-old man), so you and the elder you care for may both consider joining. It aims to eliminate the barriers between generations, and the problems facing this country's aging population. Its mission statement is "Age and youth working together," and its founding members believe that combining the experience and wisdom of age and the energy of youth can produce a powerful force for change for the better. It lobbies for better conditions for the elderly, initially concentrating on pensions, housing, drug plans, and long-term care.

As well as becoming part of what may become a powerful lobbying network, members benefit from reduced rates for travel and medical insurance and life insurance, reduced-cost prescription and over-the-counter drugs, discounts on nutritional and personal fitness consulting, and higher rates on registered and non-registered savings plans and annuities.

At the time of writing, only one chapter of the Panthers existed, but this may change in short order.

For more information, contact the Canadian Grey Panthers at 110 King Street West, Suite 685, Hamilton, Ontario L8P 4S6, or dial, toll-free, 1–800–800–7215.

Canadian Pensioners Concerned. Members of this organization are actively involved in ensuring that the concerns of their peers are heard and acted upon. CPC lobbies on behalf of older people, calling for adequate pensions, affordable housing, good long-term care, the maintenance of medicare's universality, and fair taxation policies. To this end, its members meet and correspond with members of government at all levels and band together with members of other organizations for greater impact. The organization also raises public awareness of issues affecting older people through the media, public forums, and its magazine, *Seniors' Viewpoint* (see Chapter 13).

The organization's head office rotates in line with the presidency. In other words, if the president is a member of the Nova Scotia division (which was the case at the time of writing), the head office address is that of the Nova Scotia divisional office. For more information, write to the divisional office nearest to you. There are three:

Canadian Pensioners Concerned, Alberta Division, 13923-108 Avenue, Edmonton, Alberta T5M 2C9.

Canadian Pensioners Concerned, Nova Scotia Division, Suite 310, P.O. Box 35, 7001 Mumford Road, Halifax, Nova Scotia B3L 4N9.

Canadian Pensioners Concerned, Ontario Division, 51 Bond Street, Toronto, Ontario M5B 1X1.

Connecting Seniors of Canada involves participants in health promotion programs which bring people together in groups or on a one-on-one basis. The organization builds partnerships with community-based agencies to help elders remain healthy and in their own homes. There are four programs. A Time For Me (ATFM) is complete on its own. It is a 20-hour personal growth group experience focusing on healthy aging and personal strengths. Growing Further is an unstructured peer group experience. Senior Peer Helper Training is a 50-hour program that teaches people to become volunteers who help their peers on a one-on-one basis. ATFM Co-Leader Training teaches participants how-to operate as facilitators of ATFM.

For more information, contact the organization at the Centre for Studies of Aging, University of Toronto, 455 Spadina Avenue, Suite 305, Toronto, Ontario M5S 2G8.

Dying with Dignity. The right to a good death at the end of a good life: isn't that what we would all like? But it doesn't always happen that way. The goals of Dying with Dignity are to educate people about the right to a good death—in other words, voluntary euthanasia when such a course is appropriate—and to foster greater understanding among health care professionals and the general public of the issues involved in death and dying. Its other goals include encouraging legal and medical recognition of voluntary euthanasia, and recognition and use of the living will. (A living will is a statement by the person filing it that requests medical personnel or other health care professionals not to take heroic measures or use artificial means to prolong life.)

Among services available from the organization's head office are counselling about choices for those who are terminally ill, speakers for meetings, education opportunities, and provision of living will forms and wallet cards.

For more information, contact the organization at 175 St. Clair Avenue West, Toronto, Ontario M4V 1P7.

Elderhostel Canada. This non-profit organization provides well-priced learning vacations for those aged 60 or older. (Accompanying spouses or friends can be younger than 60, but not younger than 50.) Study topics are numerous and range widely. The catalogue available at the time of writing offers an Elderhosteler a choice from among more than 400 courses. She or he might decide to explore the diverse fauna and flora around the Bay of Fundy and to study the potential consequences of tidal power development; learn the gentle art of t'ai chi while staying at an inn in Quebec's Eastern Townships; study the architecture of medieval buildings in central England; or take a course which examines in detail the political, economic, and social changes brought on in Russia by glasnost and perestroika, and possible future paths for the former Soviet Union, while staying at Ridley College in Ontario and in Moscow and St. Petersburg. A smattering of other topics to whet the appetite: birdwatching, a journey through the galaxy, the music of Oscar Peterson, mountain landscape watercolours (develop and improve your skills), early settlers' cuisine, the English country house, French language workshop (while staying in France), and famous Russian and Soviet historical figures (while staying at Ridley College and in Russia).

Elderhostel organizers manage to keep costs down in a number of ways, the most effective of which is probably arranging shared accommodation in university dormitories or in small inns or lodges with bathrooms down the hall.

For more information, write Elderhostel Canada's head office at 308 Wellington Street, Kingston, Ontario K7K 7A7, or contact your regional office as follows:

Atlantic Region
Continuing Education, Mount Saint Vincent University, 166 Bedford Highway, Halifax, Nova Scotia B3M 2J6.
British Columbia Region
Galiano Island/Therah Learning Centre, Cook Road, RR#2, Galiano Island, British Columbia V0N 1P0.
Canada North Region
510 Elliott Street, Whitehorse, Yukon Y1A 2A5.
Ontario Region
Enrichment Studies, Queen's University, Kingston, Ontario K7L 3N6.
Prairie Region
Alberta Association for Continuing Education, Box 31, Site RR#1, Priddis, Alberta T0L 1W0.
Quebec Region
P.O. Box 9843, Sainte Foy, Quebec G1V 4C3.

Federal Superannuates National Association. This organization advances, promotes, and protects the interests of retired federal government employees and retired members of the RCMP and the armed forces. It lobbies the federal government for increased allowances and full indexation of pensions, among other matters. It has 73 branches in Canada.

For more information, write the association's national office at 233 Gilmour Street, Suite 702, Ottawa, Ontario K2P 0P2.

Golden Age Association. This Montreal association has six goals: to improve its members' quality of life; to involve members in community activities, hence keeping them fit and very much in the world; to provide members with educational, recreational, social, and cultural experiences; to act as a resource and advocate for its members in their negotiations of community systems; to provide a setting in which meaningful interpersonal relationships can develop.

It has a main centre and four mini centres. Many activities take place at the main centre, among them chess, woodworking lessons, folk dances, choir performances, macramé, bridge and canasta, advanced English, Hebrew and French conversation courses, and courses in cardiopulmonary resuscitation.

The mini centres are located in Chomedey, Côte St. Luc, Dollard des Ormeaux, and St. Laurent. Activities at each of them are designed to meet the needs and interests of members. Among them: aqua exercises, swimming, line dancing, bridge lessons, games, arts and crafts, and various discussion groups.

The Centre for Creative Lifestyles, a division of the association, is home to courses in the creative arts (for example, calligraphy and watercolours), human studies (for example, current issues and the psychology of religion), and wellness (for example, exercise workouts and demystifying yoga).

As well as providing activities and services at its centres, the association has outreach programs. Its friendly visiting service sends volunteer members out to the homes of isolated elders to provide social interaction and any help needed to maintain these elders in their own homes. The tele-friend service unites volunteers with lonely, housebound elders via the telephone. In the sick visiting service, volunteers on the committee visit members who are ill in hospital and take along gifts. Project Shalom is a daily telephone service designed to ensure elders living alone or as couples are well. Elders who sign up with the association call in every day at a given time. If they fail to call, members immediately follow up to find out what, if anything, is wrong.

For more information, contact the association at 5700 Westbury Avenue, Montreal, Quebec H3W 3E8.

LIFE Institutes. LIFE is short for "learning is forever," and an institute does indeed provide opportunities for older adults to keep on learning. It sets up courses on various topics—creative writing and medical ethics are just two of many—and also may organize learning events at which experts in the topic at hand give talks. Members, who pay a modest annual fee, must be at least 50 years old.

Members taking part in courses meet once weekly

for 10 weeks. There is no teacher or lecturer, but a moderator, who is also an older adult, presides, keeping the conversation on track and moving forward, and making sure all voices are heard. Members learn not only from experts who come in to give talks, but also from doing their own research and bringing findings to the meetings, from each other, and from building upon the views or findings of other members.

LIFE institutes are modelled after similar organizations in the United States. They are relatively new in Canada. Undoubtedly they are an idea whose time has come, and chances are they will proliferate. At the time of writing, there was one in British Columbia, at Capilano College in Vancouver; three in Ontario, at Queen's University in Kingston, Laurentian University in Sudbury, and Ryerson Polytechnical Institute in Toronto; one in Quebec, at McGill University in Montreal; and one in Saskatchewan, at the University of Regina.

For more information, contact the movement's head office: LIFE Institute, 252 Victoria Street, Toronto, Ontario M5B 1V8.

Manitoba Society of Seniors Inc. This non-profit advocacy organization represents the views of Manitobans aged 55 or older to all levels of government, social service agencies, business, and the media.

MSOS also provides various services for its members. They can take advantage of a free financial counselling service; talk to a participating lawyer, who will provide a free 30-minute consultation; have a trained volunteer financial adviser prepare their income tax returns; or have Manitoba oaths, affidavits, or affirmations signed free of charge by a commissioner for oaths.

Among events organized by the society is the MSOS 55 Plus Games. Thousands of people aged 55 and older compete annually in a variety of sports and games, first, in playoffs held in all parts of the province in April and May, then—if they have succeeded—in the finals held in June. MSOS also organizes an annual walking rally called A Walk for Life Festival.

Another walking activity is Footloose and Fancy Free, a program that takes place in more than 40 indoor locations throughout the province, among them malls, arenas, and schools.

For more information, contact MSOS at 294 Portage Avenue, Suite 803, Winnipeg, Manitoba R3C 0B9, or from elsewhere in the province, call, toll-free, 1-800-561-6767.

National Pensioners and Senior Citizens Federation. The federation is a democratic, non-political, non-sectarian organization which functions as an important advocate on behalf of older Canadians. Membership comprises individuals and also 14 seniors' national and provincial organizations.

The federation's mission statement is a fivefold one. It functions as an advisory body, providing contacts, research facilities, surveys, uniform objectives, and a national expansion of the pensioners' movement.

It stimulates public interest in the provision of adequate pensions and social security that will provide comfortable housing and decent living, all this to ensure the welfare of older people.

It acts to protect the rights of those who already are or soon will be pensioners.

It works to prevent discrimination and undue delay in granting pensions.

It promotes fellowship among pensioners and older people in Canada.

Among the federation's current concerns are maintenance of the universality of Old Age Security, of health care programs across Canada, and of all other programs benefiting the elderly.

For more information, write the federation at 3033 Lakeshore Boulevard West, Toronto, Ontario M8V 1K5.

Organizations that are members of the federation, and which older people may want to join, are: Alberta Pensioners' and Senior Citizens' Organization, Fort Macleod, Alberta; Council of Senior Citizens' Organizations of British Columbia, Vancouver; Moncton Lions Senior Citizens' Club, Moncton, New Brunswick; New Brunswick Senior Citizens' Federation Inc., Moncton,

New Brunswick; Newfoundland & Labrador Senior Citizens' Federation, Marystown, Newfoundland; Nova Scotia Federation of Seniors, Amherst, Nova Scotia; Old Age Pensioners' Organization, Abbotsford, British Columbia; Old Age Pensioners' Organization, Nanaimo, British Columbia; Prince Edward Island Senior Citizens' Federation, Charlottetown, Prince Edward Island; Saskatchewan Seniors Association Inc., Sturgis, Saskatchewan; Senior Citizens Action Now, Moose Jaw, Saskatchewan; Senior Citizens Association of B.C., Revelstoke, British Columbia; Senior Citizens Coalition, Beaconsfield, Quebec; United Senior Citizens of Ontario, Toronto, Ontario.

One Voice: The Canadian Seniors Network. This national, non-profit organization works to improve conditions for those aged 65 or older, and provides a network linking older people right across Canada and keeping them informed. It addresses national issues of interest or concern to elders and presents their point of view to decision makers in government, business, and industry. It represents elders' interests to the federal government, presenting their concerns and ensuring that their voices are heard. Above all, it is a network, putting members in touch with one another and keeping them informed through its publications and through the conferences, workshops, opinion surveys, and consultations it holds regularly.

For more information, write to One Voice at 350 Sparks Street, Suite 1005, Ottawa, Ontario K1R 7S8.

Prince Edward Island Senior Citizens' Federation. The federation's main objective is to further the interests and promote the happiness and welfare of older people living in Prince Edward Island. It seeks funding to respond to the needs of older people, runs informative workshops, meets with members of government to express concerns regarding services and programs necessary for elderly people, and conducts research and disseminates its findings. Anyone living on the island who is 50 or older may join the federation. The spouse of a member may join even if she or he is not yet 50.

For more information, write to the federation at P.O. Box 152, Charlottetown, Prince Edward Island C1A 7K4.

Royal Canadian Legion. With close to 600,000 members, the Royal Canadian Legion is by far the largest veterans' organization in the country. It is non-profit and has 1,750 branches right across Canada. Membership is open to all veterans and to serving and former members of the Canadian armed forces and their dependents.

The Legion works in many ways to better the lot of elders. Each year it awards eight fellowships, four to medical doctors and four to nurses, to pursue postgraduate studies in geriatrics. It sponsors meals on wheels programs, vehicles to transport those in wheelchairs and those with other disabilities to and from day hospitals, telephone assurance programs, home handyperson help, and escort or transportation services for shopping and appointments. It has built homes for elders in many centres, as well as a retirement home in Vancouver. It makes its club premises available to elders' clubs on a regular basis.

For more information, contact your local branch of the Legion.

Second Mile Club. This organization providing those aged 55 and older with social and recreational activities is at six locations in Metro Toronto. The club also operates an Enhanced Program for the Elderly and a daycare service for the frail elderly available three days a week.

For more information, contact the club's head office at 110 Edward Street, Toronto, Ontario M5G 2A5.

Ulyssean Society. Members of this chartered, nonprofit society are dedicated to the fact that men and women in their middle and later years can produce, learn, and create just as effectively as younger people, and can continue to do so until the end of their lives. So far, there is the founding chapter of the society in Toronto, and one in Niagara-on-the-Lake, Ontario. But this is another idea whose time has clearly come, and more chapters may come into being in the future.

Members (known as Companions) participate in several activities. They meet once monthly to hear guest speakers and to ask questions of them. Speakers' topics range widely. A brief sampling includes film and national identity, Mozart and his times, an open letter to Carl Sagan, and confessions of a ghost writer for Pierre Trudeau.

Members also join interest groups and attend their meetings. Groups' areas of interest are indicated by their names: Armchair Travel, Cosmic Trails, Music Appreciation, Playreading, Guild of Servers, Social Concerns and Human Needs, and T'ai Chi. The President's Open Circle meets for general discussion.

Groups of members also attend plays, concerts, films, and museum and planetarium events.

There are no age restrictions for membership in the society. Most members are between their mid-40s and mid-80s; of these, most are somewhere between 55 and 75.

For more information, contact the Secretary, Ulysean Society, 215 Richview Avenue, Toronto, Ontario M5P 3G2.

CHAPTER THIRTEEN

GOING TO THE SOURCE

FURTHER READING AND VIEWING

This list of suggested further reading and viewing materials is by no means exhaustive. As the number of elders in Canadian society has increased, so have the number of books, periodicals, other printed materials, and videos on various aspects of aging and caregiving.

Note that only the head office cities of the organizations are shown. Many of these organizations, such as the Canadian National Institute for the Blind and the National Film Board, are pleased to provide materials through their local branches. If you would like to rent NFB videos, you may call, toll-free: Atlantic Canada 1-800-561-7104, Quebec 1-800-363-0328, Ontario 1-800-267-7710, and western and northern Canada 1-800-661-9867.

Note also that if the nature of an item listed is not specified (e.g., video, booklet), but its title is preceded by a person or group's name, the item is a book.

Some of the books listed may now be out of print. But your local public library, a rich resource centre, will almost certainly have them. It will probably also have some of the videos on exercise and nutrition.

General Reading and Viewing

About Occupational Therapy. Booklet. Canadian Association of Occupational Therapists, Toronto, Ontario.

aca News. Bimonthly magazine. Alberta Council on Aging, Edmonton, Alberta.

Adler, Mark, and Janis Rotman. *$enior$ $aving$*. Toronto, Ontario: Redeagle Publishing Ltd.

Bulletin. Quarterly newsletter. The Canadian Red Cross Society, Ontario Division, Mississauga, Ontario.

CARP News. Quarterly tabloid. Kemur Publishing Co. Ltd., North York, Ontario.

Canada News. Weekly tabloid. Rennie Printing & Publishing Ltd., St. Catharines, Ontario.

Cheney, Walter J., William J. Diehm, and Frank E. Seeley. *The Second 50 Years: A Reference Manual for Senior Citizens*. New York: Paragon House Publishers, 1992. (Note: This is an American book; some sections, including several on medical assistance, insurance, and finance, contain information that is not germane to a Canadian reader. However, with a total of 433 sections, the book contains much information that *is* relevant for Canadians.)

Comfort, Alex. *Say Yes to Old Age: Developing a Positive*

Attitude Toward Aging. New York: Crown Publishers Inc.

Discover Choices. A kit comprising 23 articles on many aspects of aging, most of them written by elders, and guides to resources for elders in Manitoba and Saskatchewan. Health and Welfare Canada.

Don't Take My Sunshine Away. National Film Board Video No. C 91919 113.

Dychtwald, Ken, and Joe Flower. *Age Wave: The Challenges and Opportunities of an Aging North America*. Los Angeles: J.P. Tarcher, 1989.

Edmonton Senior, The. Tabloid issued six times annually. Alberta Business Research Ltd., Edmonton, Alberta.

Elder Abuse: The Hidden Scourge. Booklet. Manitoba Society of Seniors Inc., Winnipeg, Manitoba.

Elder Statesman. Monthly tabloid. Today's Times Publications Ltd., Vancouver, British Columbia.

Entre Nous. Quarterly newsletter. The Toronto Ulyssean Society, Toronto, Ontario.

Expression. Quarterly bulletin. The National Advisory Council on Aging, Ottawa, Ontario.

50 Plus. Monthly tabloid. Insight Publications, Durham, Ontario.

Fifty-Five Plus. Magazine issued six times annually. Limestone City Publications, Battersea, Ontario.

Foresight. Bimonthly magazine. Trustor Ltd., Montreal, Quebec.

Good Times. Magazine issued ten times annually. Senior Publications Inc., Montreal, Quebec.

Gordon, Dr. Michael. *Old Enough to Feel Better: A Medical Guide for Seniors*. Baltimore: Johns Hopkins University Press, 1989.

Health After 50. The Johns Hopkins monthly medical newsletter. Medletter Associates Palm Coast, Florida, U.S.A.

Horizons. Monthly tabloid. Laurentian Publishing, Sudbury, Ontario.

Housing Choices for Older Canadians. Handbook. Canada Mortgage and Housing Corporation.

Housing for Older Canadians: New Financial and Tenure Options. Handbook. Canada Mortgage and Housing Corporation.

Independent Senior, The. Tabloid issued ten times annually. K.W. Publishing Ltd., Vancouver, British Columbia.

Just Grand. Quarterly digest. Maturity Communications Inc., Surrey, British Columbia.

Legion. Monthly magazine. Canvet Publications Ltd., Ottawa, Ontario.

Live It Up! A Guide to Healthy Active Living in the Senior Years. Health promotion kit with articles for both caregivers and elders. ParticipACTION, Toronto, Ontario.

Living with Dying. National Film Board Video No. C 9191 037.

MSOS *Journal*. Tabloid issued eleven times annually. Manitoba Society of Seniors Inc., Winnipeg, Manitoba.

Mainly for Seniors. Monthly magazine. Leader Publications Ltd., Petrolia, Ontario.

Maintaining Seniors' Independence: A Guide to Home Adaptations. Handbook. Canada Mortgage and Housing Corporation.

Maturity. Quarterly magazine. Maturity Communications Inc., Surrey, British Columbia.

McLeish, John A.B. *The Challenge of Aging: Ulyssean Paths to Creative Living*. Vancouver: Douglas and McIntyre, 1983.

Ministry of Health, British Columbia. *Choosing Wellness: An Approach to Healthy Aging*. Ministry of Health, British Columbia.

Molloy, Dr. William. *Vital Choices: Life, Death and the Health Care Crisis*. Markham, Ont.: Penguin Books Canada Ltd.

Molloy, Dr. William, and Virginia Mepham. *Let Me Decide: The Health Care Directive That Speaks for You When You Can't*. Markham, Ont.: Penguin Books Canada Ltd., 1992.

Muskoka Seniors News. Tabloid issued six times annually. Muskoka Publications Group, Bracebridge, Ontario.

National Network. Quarterly newsletter. VON Canada, Ottawa, Ontario.

Natural Healing Newsletter. Monthly newsletter. FC&A Publishing, Peachtree City, Georgia, U.S.A.

News for Seniors. Monthly magazine. Trend Publications (Calgary) Ltd., Edmonton, Alberta.

Novak, Dr. Mark. *Successful Aging: The Myths, Realities and Future of Aging in Canada*. Markham, Ont.: Penguin Books Canada Ltd., 1985.

Peninsula Prime. Monthly magazine. The Peace Arch News, White Rock, British Columbia.

Pension Primer, A. A report by the National Council of Welfare, Ottawa, Ontario.

Pitzele, Sefra Kobin. *We Are Not Alone: Learning to Live with Chronic Illness*. Workman Publishing, 1986.

Retirement Lifestyle. Magazine issued ten times annually. Club 55 Directories Inc., Vancouver, British Columbia.

Senior Times, The. Biweekly newspaper. Publications Newborn Inc., Montreal, Quebec.

Seniors Choice, The. Monthly tabloid. Egress Enterprises Inc., Kelowna, British Columbia.

Seniors Info Exchange. Quarterly newsletter. Seniors Secretariat, Health and Welfare Canada.

Seniors on the Move. Monthly magazine. 933951 Ontario Ltd., Barrie, Ontario.

Seniors' Viewpoint. Quarterly newsletter. Canadian Pensioners Concerned Inc., Ontario Division, Toronto, Ontario.

Something to Celebrate. National Film Board Video No. C 0183 023.

Today's Seniors. Monthly tabloid. Metroland Printing, Publishing & Distributing, Mississauga, Ontario.

Underwood, Richard D., and Brenda Breeden Underwood. *Wise & Healthy Living: A Commonsense Approach for Aging Well.* Vancouver: International Self-Counsel Press, 1989.

West, Michelle. *Seniority: In Search of the Best in Nursing Homes & Alternative Care in Canada.* Don Mills, Ont.: Addison-Wesley Publishers Ltd., 1991.

Westcoast Reflections. Monthly magazine. Westcoast Publishing Ltd., Victoria, British Columbia.

Wigdor, Blossom, with Arthur Drache. *Planning Your Retirement: The Complete Self-Help Guide.* Toronto: Grosvenor House Press Inc., 1985.

Wigdor, Blossom, and David K. Foot. *The Over-Forty Society: Issues for Canada's Aging Population.* Toronto: James Lorimer & Co., 1988.

Physical Problems

Abilities: Canada's Lifestyle Magazine for People with Disabilities. Quarterly magazine. Canadian Abilities Foundation, Toronto, Ontario.

All About Epilepsy. Video. Local epilepsy associations or Epilepsy Ontario, North York, Ontario.

Arthritis News. Quarterly magazine. The Arthritis Society, Toronto. (A French version is called *Communiqué.*)

Asthma Handbook, The. Booklet. The Lung Association, Toronto, Ontario.

Back Basics. Booklet. The Back Association of Canada, Toronto, Ontario.

Back to Back. Quarterly journal. The Back Association of Canada, Toronto, Ontario.

Blau, Sheldon, and Dodi Schultz. *Lupus: The Body Against Itself.* Garden City, N.Y.: Doubleday and Co. Inc., 1977.

Burgio, Kathryn L. *Staying Dry: A Practical Guide to Bladder Control.* Baltimore: Johns Hopkins University Press, 1989.

Calne, Susan. *Parkinson's Disease—What Now?* Vancouver: University of British Columbia Press, 1991.

CCFC *Journal, The.* Quarterly newsletter. Crohn's and Colitis Foundation of Canada, Toronto, Ontario.

Communiqué. Twice yearly newsletter. The Canadian Liver Foundation, Toronto, Ontario.

Courier. Three times yearly newsletter. The Kidney Foundation, Toronto, Ontario.

Crawford, Irene. *Aids to Independence: A Guide to Products for the Disabled and Elderly.* Vancouver: International Self-Counsel Press, 1985.

Cunningham, Alastair J. *The Healing Journey: Overcoming the Crisis of Cancer.* Toronto: Key Porter Books Ltd., 1992.

Diabetes and Seniors. Booklet. Canadian Diabetes Association, Toronto, Ontario.

Diabetes Dialogue. Quarterly magazine. Canadian Diabetes Association, Toronto, Ontario.

Diabetes Over 60: Meals to Serve You Well. Booklet. Canadian Diabetes Association, Toronto, Ontario.

Disability Today. Quarterly magazine. Disability Today Publishing Group, Inc., St. Catharines, Ontario.

Disease No One Wants to Talk About, The. Video. Crohn's and Colitis Foundation of Canada, Toronto, Ontario.

Dollinger, Dr. Malin, Dr. Ernest H. Rosenbaum, and Greg Cable. *Everyone's Guide to Cancer Therapy: How Cancer Is Diagnosed, Treated, and Managed Day to Day.* Toronto: Somerville House Books Ltd., 1991.

Drug Therapy of Inflammatory Bowel Disease. Leaflet. Crohn's and Colitis Foundation of Canada, Toronto, Ontario.

Exercise and Diabetes. Booklet. Canadian Diabetes Association, Toronto, Ontario.

Fine, Judylaine. *Conquering Back Pain.* Toronto: Prentice-Hall Canada Inc., 1987.

Fries, James F., MD. *Arthritis: A Comprehensive Guide to Understanding Your Arthritis.* Reading, Mass.: Addison-Wesley Publishing Co., 1990.

Foot Owner's Manual, A. Booklet. The Canadian Diabetes Association, Toronto, Ontario.

Gartley, Cheryle B., ed. *Managing Incontinence: A Guide*

to Living with Loss of Bladder Control. Toronto: The Simon Foundation of Canada, 1985.

Gumnit, Robert J., MD. *Living Well with Epilepsy*. New York: Demos Publications, 1989.

Hauser, W. Allen, MD, and Dale C. Hesdorffer, MPH. *Epilepsy: Frequency, Causes and Consequences*. New York: Demos Publications, 1990.

HeartCare package. Includes a video, a book, a progress journal, and sample recipes. The Heart and Stroke Foundation of Ontario, Toronto. Available in bookstores and selected pharmacies, or call 1-800-268-1121.

HeartHealth. Quarterly newsletter. The Heart and Stroke Foundation of Canada, Ottawa, Ontario.

Help Yourself to Better Breathing. Handbook. The Lung Association, Toronto, Ontario.

Hopkins, Anthony. *Epilepsy: The Facts*. Oxford University Press.

Horner, Pamela. *Osteoporosis: The Long Road Back*. Ottawa: University of Ottawa Press.

Hutton, J. Thomas, MD, PhD, and Raye Lynne Dipple, PhD, eds. *Caring for the Parkinson Patient: A Practical Guide*. Buffalo, N.Y.: Prometheus Books, 1989.

Informer, The. Quarterly newsletter. The Simon Foundation of Canada, Toronto, Ontario.

Johnson, Alan G., and David R. Triger. *Liver Disease and Gallstones*. New York: Oxford University Press, 1987.

Kavanagh, Dr. Terence. *Take Heart*. Toronto: Key Porter Books Ltd., 1992.

Liver, The. Video. The Canadian Liver Foundation, Toronto, Ontario.

Living with Crohn's Disease. Video. Crohn's and Colitis Foundation of Canada, Toronto, Ontario.

Living with Kidney Disease. Manual. The Kidney Foundation of Canada, Montreal, Quebec.

Living with Ulcerative Colitis. Video. Crohn's and Colitis Foundation of Canada, Toronto, Ontario.

Living with Vision Loss. Video. Canadian National Institute for the Blind, Toronto, Ontario.

Lorig, Kate, RN, DrPH., and James S. Fries, MD. *The Arthritis Helpbook*. Addison-Wesley Publishing Company, 1990.

McGinn, Kerry Anne. *The Ostomy Book for Nurses*. Palo Alto, California: Bull Publishing Co., 1985.

Mullen, Barbara Dorr, and Kerry Anne McGinn. *The Ostomy Book*. Bull Publishing Co., 1992.

Naeyaert, Kathleen, and Jessie Love. *Living with Vision Loss: A Handbook for Caregivers*. Canadian National Institute for the Blind, Toronto, Ontario.

Network. Five times annually newsletter. The Parkinson Foundation of Canada, Toronto, Ontario.

Newsletter. Monthly. Canadian Council of the Blind, Ottawa, Ontario.

Nothing I Can't Do. Video. United Ostomy Association of Canada.

Osteoporosis: Basic Exercise Program. Video. Osteoporosis Society of Canada.

Other Diabetes, The: Your Guide to Living with Non-Insulin Dependent (Type II) Diabetes. Booklet. The Canadian Diabetes Association, Toronto, Ontario.

Pathways to Independence. Video. Canadian National Institute for the Blind.

Phillips, Robert H. *Coping with an Ostomy*. Wayne, N.J.: Avery Publishing Group, 1986.

Psychological Aspects of Inflammatory Bowel Disease. Leaflet. Crohn's and Colitis Foundation of Canada, Toronto, Ontario.

Questions about Crohn's Disease and Ulcerative Colitis. Leaflet. Crohn's and Colitis Foundation of Canada, Toronto, Ontario.

Reflections on Suffering. National Film Board Video No. C 0182.

Rehabilitation Digest. Quarterly Magazine. The Canadian Rehabilitation Council for the Disabled, Toronto, Ontario.

Svoboda, William B. *Learning about Epilepsy*. University Park Press.

Toogood, Dr. John, and Dr. Jean-Luc Malo. *Every Breath You Take: Coping with Asthma and Other Respiratory Diseases*. Toronto: Grosvenor House Press, 1989.

Vibrations. Quarterly magazine. The Canadian Hearing Society, Toronto, Ontario.

Why Not? Booklet. The Parkinson Foundation of Canada, Toronto, Ontario.

Psychological Problems

Please note that items followed by an asterisk may be available through your local Alzheimer office. If you wish to discuss the book or video beforehand, contact the provincial or national office of the Alzheimer Society of Canada.

Alzheimer Disease: A Handbook for Care. Alzheimer Society of Canada, Toronto, Ontario.

Alzheimer's Disease: A Family Information Handbook. Health and Welfare Canada.

Alzheimer's Disease: Pieces of the Puzzle. Five videos. Arizona Health Sciences Centre, Tucson, Arizona.*

Alzheimer's 101: The Basics for Caregiving. Video. South Carolina, ETV, Columbia, South Carolina.

AlzheimeRapport. Quarterly newsletter. Alzheimer Society of Canada, Toronto, Ontario.

Best They Can Be, The: Communicating with People Who Have Alzheimer Disease. Alzheimer's: A Delicate Balance. Alzheimer Disease and the Family: The Real Victims. Alzheimer's: No Easy Answers. Building Upon the Strengths. Videos. Metro Toronto Homes for the Aged.

Canada Mortgage and Housing Corporation. *At Home with Alzheimer's Disease: Useful Adaptations to the*

Home Environment. Canada Mortgage and Housing Corporation.*

Caregiver Series. Five videos. Alzheimer's Disease and Related Disorders Association, Chicago, Illinois.*

CMHA *National*. Quarterly newsletter. The Canadian Mental Health Association, Toronto, Ontario.

Cohen, Donna, and Carl Eisdorfer. *The Loss of Self*. Markham, Ont.: Penguin Books Canada Ltd.

Cohen, Uriel, and Gerald D. Weisman. *Holding on to Home: Designing Environments for People with Dementia*. Baltimore: Johns Hopkins University Press.*

Dementia and Activities of Daily Living: A Report on Technologies and Environmental Design That Can Assist People with Alzheimer Disease and Related Dementias. Ontario Ministry of Community and Social Services.*

Designing Facilities for People with Dementia. Health and Welfare Canada.*

Forbes Home, The. National Film Board Video No. C 0182084.

Freeman, Sally. *Activities and Approaches for Alzheimer's*. Whitfield Agency.*

Glickstein, Joan K. *Therapeutic Interventions in Alzheimer's Disease: A Program of Functional Communication Skills for Activities of Daily Living*. Aspen Publishers.*

Guidelines for Care. Booklet. Alzheimer Society of Canada, Toronto, Ontario.

Kociol, Lori, and Myra Schiff. *Alzheimer: A Canadian*

Family Resource Guide. Toronto: McGraw-Hill Ryerson, 1989.

Mace, Nancy L., and Peter V. Rabins. *The 36-Hour Day: A Family Guide to Caring for Persons with Alzheimer's Disease, Related Dementing Illnesses, and Memory Loss in Later Life*. Baltimore: Johns Hopkins University Press, 1981.

Mental Health in Later Years. Booklet. Health and Welfare Canada.

Nissenboim, Sylvia, and Christine Vroman. *Interactions by Design: The Positive Interactions Program for Persons with Alzheimer's Disease and Related Disorders*. St. Louis, Missouri: Geri-Active Consultants, 1989.*

Ontario Ministry of Community and Social Services. *My House Is Not My Home: Practical Technology to Make the Home Safe and Manageable for Persons with Dementia*. Senior Care, Toronto.*

Robinson, Ann, and Beth Spender. *Understanding Difficult Behaviors: Some Practical Suggestions for Coping with Alzheimer's Disease and Related Illnesses*. Eastern Michigan University Press.

Sachter, Marlene. *The Happy Book for Special People*. Self-published by the author and available through the Alzheimer Society for Metropolitan Toronto.

Sheridan, Carmel. *Failure-Free Activities for the Alzheimer's Patient: A Guidebook for Caregivers*. Oakland, California: Cottage Books, 1987.*

Sonia. National Film Board Video No. C 10186 052.

Zgola, Jitka M. *Doing Things: A Guide to Programming Activities for Persons with Alzheimer's Disease and Related Disorders.* Baltimore: Johns Hopkins University Press, 1987.

Medications

Canadian Medical Association Guide to Prescription and Over-the-Counter Drugs, The. The Reader's Digest Association (Canada) Ltd.

Griffith, H. Winter. *Complete Guide to Prescription and Non-Prescription Drugs: Side Effects, Warnings and Vital Data for Safe Use.* New York: The Body Press, 1993.

Medicated Generation, The. Video. Parke-Davis Canada Inc., Toronto, Ontario.

Pills Unlimited. National Film Board Video No. C 9190 136.

Prescription Drugs, A Home Health Handbook by the Editors of Consumer Guide. Publications International Ltd.

Smith, Dorothy L. *Understanding Canadian Prescription Drugs: A Consumer's Guide to Correct Use.* Toronto: Key Porter Books Ltd., 1992.

Wolfe, Sidney M., Lisa Fugate, Elizabeth P. Hulstrand, Laurie E. Kamimoto, and the Public Citizen Health Research Group. *Worst Pills, Best Pills: The Older Adult's Guide to Avoiding Drug-Induced Death or Illness.*

Washington, D.C.: Public Citizen Health Research Group, 1988.

Caregivers' Guides

Ahronheim, Judith C. *Final Passages: Positive Choices for the Dying and Their Loved Ones*. New York: Simon and Schuster, 1992.

Brody, Elaine. *Women in the Middle: Their Parent-Care Years*. New York: Springer Publishing Co., 1990.

Buckman, Robert. *I Don't Know What to Say: How to Help and Support Someone Who Is Dying*. Toronto: Key Porter Books Ltd., 1988.

Duda, Deborah. *Coming Home: A Guide to Dying at Home with Dignity*. Aurora Press.

Felder, Leonard. *When a Loved One Is Ill: How to Take Better Care of Your Loved One, Your Family and Yourself*. New York: Plume, 1991.

Koch, Tom. *A Place in Time: Care Givers for Their Elderly*. Praeger Publishers.

Kübler-Ross, Elisabeth. *Living with Death and Dying*. New York: Macmillan, 1981.

Last Days of Living, The. National Film Board Video No. C 0185 112.

McCarthy, Sherri. *A Death in the Family: A Self-Help Guide to Coping with Grief*. Vancouver: Self-Counsel Press, 1988.

McLean, Helene. *Caring for Your Parents: A Sourcebook*

of Options and Solutions for Both Generations. Doubleday Ltd.

My Mother, My Father. Video. Canadian Learning Co., Scarborough, Ontario.

Pearsall, Paul. *The Power of the Family: Strength, Comfort and Healing*. Toronto: Doubleday Canada Ltd., 1990.

Priory, The Only Home I've Got. National Film Board Video No. C 0182 045.

Rhodes, Ann. *Guidance and Support in Caring for the Elderly*. Montreal: Grosvenor House Press, published in association with the Canadian Medical Association, 1989.

Silverstone, Barbara, and Helen Kandel Hyman. *You and Your Aging Parent*. New York: Pantheon Books, 1982.

Thompson, Wendy. *Aging Is a Family Affair: A Guide to Quality Visiting, Long-Term Care Facilities and You*. Toronto: NC Press Ltd., 1990.

Time for Caring, A. National Film Board Video No. C 0182 045.

Watt, Jill, and Ann Calder. *Taking Care: A Self-Help Guide for Coping with an Elderly, Chronically Ill, or Disabled Relative*. Vancouver: International Self-Counsel Press, 1986.

When the Day Comes. National Film Board Video No. C 9190 139.

Wylie, Betty Jean. *New Beginnings: Living Through Loss and Grief*. Toronto: Key Porter Books Ltd., 1991.

Exercise and Nutrition

Age Is No Barrier. National Film Board Video No. C 9189 075.

Blais, C. *Aging Into the Twenty-First Century*. North York, Ont.: Captus University Publications, 1991.

Brody, Jane E. *Jane Brody's Nutrition Book*. New York: Norton, 1981.

Canada's Food Guide Handbook. Health and Welfare Canada.

Common Sense Nutrition for Seniors. Handbook: includes recipes. Ontario Ministry of Agriculture and Food.

Controlling Cholesterol: After 50. Video. Zadox Inc., New York.

Controlling Cholesterol: Through Diet and Nutrition. Video. Zadox Inc., New York.

Exercise with Billie: Chair Exercises to Keep You Moving. Video. Princeton Book Co., Pennington, New Jersey.

Harris, R., and L. Frankel. *Guide to Fitness After Fifty*. New York: Plenum Press, 1977.

Harris, R., and S. Harris. *Physical Activity, Aging and Sports*, vols. 1 and 2. Center for the Study of Aging, 1989.

Hollands, Marjorie, and Margaret Howard. *Choice Menus: An Easy Guide with Recipes for Healthy Everyday Meal Planning*. Toronto: Macmillan of Canada, published in association with the Canadian Diabetes Association, 1993.

It Works For Us! A Guide to Healthful Eating for Older Adults. Canadian Pensioners Concerned Inc., Metropolitan Toronto Chapter.

Kowalski, Robert E. *The 8-Week Cholesterol Cure: How to Lower Your Blood Cholesterol by up to 40 Percent Without Drugs or Deprivation*. New York: Harper & Row, 1989.

Lindsay, Anne. *The Lighthearted Cookbook: Recipes for Healthy Heart Cooking*. Toronto: Key Porter Books Ltd., 1988.

Lindsay, Anne. *Low-Cholesterol Cuisine: Gourmet Eating the Low-Cholesterol Way with Over 200 Fast, Easy and Great-Tasting Recipes for a Healthy Heart*. Hearst Books.

MacDonald, Helen Bishop. *Eating for the Health of It: A New Look at Nutrition*. Austin Books.

MacDonald, Helen Bishop, and Margaret Howard. *Eat Well, Live Well: The Canadian Dietetic Association's Guide to Healthy Eating*. Toronto: Macmillan of Canada, 1990.

Metric Measures. Booklet. Canadian Diabetes Association, Toronto, Ontario.

Oliver, Margo. *Margo Oliver's Cookbook for Seniors: Nutritious Recipes for One, Two or More*. Vancouver: International Self-Counsel Press, 1989.

Shephard, R.J. *Physical Activity and Aging*, second edition. Croom Helm Publishing.

Shephard, R.J., and S.G. Thomas. *Fit After Fifty: Feel*

Better Live Longer. Vancouver: International Self-Counsel Retirement Series, 1989.

Shopping Heart Smart. Video. Heart and Stroke Foundation of Canada, Ottawa, Ontario.

Smith, E.L., and R.C. Serfass. *Exercise and Aging: The Scientific Basis*. Enslow Press.

Spirduso, W.W., and H.M. Eckert. *The Academy Papers: Physical Activity and Aging*. Human Kinetics Publishers.

Walker, Sheila, and Beverly Renahan. *Healthy Choices: Everyday Recipes for Healthy Eating*. Macmillan of Canada, published in association with the Canadian Diabetes Association.

Wesler, Cathy A., ed. *Cooking Light Cookbook 1993*. Toronto: Fitzhenry & Whiteside Ltd., 1993.

Finding Services

Mr. Nobody. National Film Board Video No. X 0187 100.

Seniors' Guide to Federal Programs and Services. Handbook. Health and Welfare Canada.

Services and Benefits. Booklet. Veterans Affairs Canada.

Most provinces and territories have one or more booklets and/or leaflets giving details of programs and services available for elders. All are free of charge. Typical content? Sections on retirement income from both federal and provincial sources; health benefits and services;

helping services; housing services, including grants; recreational programs; transportation; legal services; organizations for elders. Here's a listing of booklets and where you can obtain them.

Alberta

Programs for Seniors, available from the Seniors Advisory Council for Alberta, Room 405, Energy Square, 10109 106 Street, Edmonton, Alta. T5J 3L7.

British Columbia

Information for Seniors: Your Guide to Programs & Benefits in British Columbia, available from the Office for Seniors, Ministry of Health and Ministry Responsible for Seniors, 6-2, 1515 Blanshard Street, Victoria, B.C. V8W 3C9.

Manitoba

Manitoba Senior Citizens' Handbook, available from the Manitoba Council on Aging, 333-260 St. Mary Avenue, Winnipeg, Man. R3C 0M6.

New Brunswick

Seniors' Guide to Services and Programs, available from the Office for Seniors, Department of Health and Community Services, P.O. Box 5100, Fredericton, N.B. E3B 5G8.

Newfoundland and Labrador

No up-to-date provincial elders' guide. Literature on various programs and services available from the Seniors Resource Centre, Suite 104, Prince Charles Building, 120 Torbay Road, St. John's, Nfld. A1A 2G8.

Northwest Territories

Programs and Services for Senior Citizens, available from the Department of Social Services, Government of the N.W.T., Precambrian Building, Box 1320, Yellowknife, NWT X1A 2L9.

Nova Scotia

Programs for Seniors, available from the Senior Citizens' Secretariat, P.O. Box 2065, Halifax, N.S. B3J 2Z1.

Ontario

The Guide for Senior Citizens: Services and Programs in Ontario, available from the Office for Seniors' Issues, Ministry of Citizenship, 76 College Street, Queen's Park, Toronto, Ont. M7A 1N3.

Prince Edward Island

Services for Seniors on Prince Edward Island, available from the Minister Responsible for the Elderly, Department of Health and Social Services, P.O. Box 2000, Charlottetown, P.E.I. C1A 7N8.

Quebec

No up-to-date provincial elders' guide. Literature available from various community organizations such as the Golden Age Association and Community Information Services in Montreal.

Saskatchewan

Directory of Programs and Services for Persons with Disabilities, and leaflets on individual aspects of aging and programs, all available from the Seniors' Secretariat, 2151 Scarth Street, Regina, Sask. S4P 3Z3.

Yukon

A Handbook for Seniors: Information Please . . . available from the Seniors Information Centre, 3 106 Main Street, Whitehorse, Yukon Y1A 2A8.

ORGANIZATIONS OFFERING INFORMATION AND COUNSEL

As well as consulting the reading and viewing materials listed above to glean more information about various aspects of aging and caregiving, you can also call upon a number of organizations for more facts and counsel. You would be wise do so when necessary: the caregiver role you have taken upon yourself is not always an easy one and, not least because of heavy demands on their time, most caregivers need all the help they can get.

Before starting on the list of organizations, here are two other listings you may well need.

First, you should be aware that you can obtain information from the federal government. A service known as Reference Canada has several toll-free numbers staffed by officers who will be pleased to help you track down information. For all provinces and territories, with the exception of Manitoba and Quebec, dial 1-800-667-3355. For Manitoba, dial 1-800-282-8060; if in Winnipeg, dial 945-3744. For Quebec, dial 1-800-363-9883; if in Montreal, dial 873-2111, and if in Hull, dial 772-3232.

Second, if you want to know more about provincial and territorial services for the elderly, you should write to or telephone your provincial or territorial seniors' secretariat. Here are their addresses:

Alberta

Services to Seniors Division, Seventh Street Plaza, 10030 107th Street, 10th Floor, Edmonton, Alta. T5J 3E4.

British Columbia

Office for Seniors, Ministry of Health, 1515 Blanshard Street, 6th Floor, Victoria, B.C. V8W 3C8.

Manitoba

Manitoba Seniors Directorate, 450 500 Portage Avenue, Winnipeg, Man. R3C 3X1. Toll-free 1-800-665-6565.

New Brunswick

Office for Seniors, Department of Health and Community Services, 520 King Street, 4th Floor, P.O. Box 5100, Fredericton, N.B. E3B 5G8.

Newfoundland

Division of Services to Senior Citizens, Department of Health, West Block, Confederation Building, P.O. Box 8700, St. John's, Nfld. A1B 4J6.

Northwest Territories

Extended Health Benefits Program for Seniors, Health Insurance Services Division, Box 1320, Yellowknife, NWT X1A 2L9. Zenith 06025 (no charge if calling from anywhere in the Northwest Territories). Also

Coordinator, Aged and Handicapped, Community and Family Support Services, at the same address.

Nova Scotia

Nova Scotia Senior Citizens' Secretariat, 1740 Granville Street, 4th Floor, P.O. Box 2065, Halifax, N.S. B3J 2Z1. Toll-free 1-800-424-0065.

Ontario

Office for Seniors' Issues, Ministry of Citizenship, 76 College Street, 6th Floor, Toronto, Ont. M7A 1N3. Toll-free 1-800-267-7329.

Prince Edward Island

Division of Aging and Extended Care, Department of Health and Social Services, P.O. Box 2000, Charlottetown, P.E.I. C1A 7N8.

Quebec

Ministry of Health and Social Services, Joffre Building, 1075 Ste-Foy, 4th Floor, Quebec City, Que. G1S 2M1. Toll-free 1-800-361-0635.

Saskatchewan

Saskatchewan Seniors' Secretariat, 2151 Scarth Street, Regina, Sask. S4P 3Z3. Toll-free 1-800-667-7161.

Yukon

Department of Health and Social Services, Government of Yukon, P.O. Box 2703, Whitehorse, Yukon Y1A 2C6. Toll-free 1-800-661-0408.

Now here, in alphabetical order, is the list of other organizations you may want to call upon for information and/or counsel:

Canadian Dietetic Association. Some 5,000 dietitians belong to this association. If you need to find a dietitian near you, it can supply contacts. Write the association at 480 University Avenue, Suite 601, Toronto, Ontario M5G 1V2.

Canadian Rehabilitation Council for the Disabled. If you need any information about helping or caring for someone with a disability, personnel at the council can put you in touch with its member in your area. It has a member in every province. Write the council at 45 Sheppard Avenue East, Suite 801, Toronto, Ontario M2N 5W9.

National Advisory Council on Aging. NACA has several priorities, among them promoting learning in later life, encouraging educators to develop programs to train people who will work with and for the elderly, encouraging educators to make sure there is material on aging when they are developing new courses, and helping groups (both public and private) to become aware of the potential and needs of older workers. Since NACA personnel consult on a regular basis with elders and with all kinds of groups concerned with aging and issues affecting the elderly, staff members have a wealth of information to impart on numerous topics having to do with aging and the elderly. At the time of writing, the council's address was 473 Albert Street, Room 355, Ottawa, Ontario K1A 0K9. However, the federal government had recently announced that, in order to cut costs, the council would merge with the National Council of Welfare—a merger which reflects sadly (and too accurately) the government's view as to elders' finances in general. Since NACA consults regularly with the Minister of National Health and Welfare, inquire at your local Health and Welfare office in case there has been a change of address.

Secretariat for Fitness in the Third Age. If you need any information about active living and fitness for older people, write to the secretariat at 1600 James Naismith Drive, Suite 312, Gloucester, Ontario K1B 5N4, or call toll-free 1-800-361-2756.

Senior Talent Bank Association of Ontario. Senior talent banks are groups of older volunteers who work with other elderly people in the community, helping them to find new roles and purposes, as well as chances to share knowledge, talents, and experiences. They thus remain active and a force for good in the community. At the time of writing there were 12 senior talent banks in Ontario; personnel at the association can advise you if there is one in or near your community. As well, if an elder you care for would like to start a talent bank, the association has a how-to manual outlining the steps to take. Write the association at 55 Belmont Street, Toronto, Ontario M5R 1R1, or call toll-free 1-800-263-0223.

Seniors Secretariat, Health and Welfare Canada. Secretariat staff consult on an ongoing basis with federal government departments and agencies to coordinate and foster programs and policies for the elderly. As well, they consult with provincial governments and with seniors' organizations, professional groups, and voluntary associations. They are, therefore, a good source of information for anyone needing to know about any services and benefits available to older Canadians. Write to the secretariat at Health and Welfare Canada, 473 Albert Street, 3rd Floor, Ottawa, Ontario K1A 0K9.

MY SOURCES

Name of organization	*Name of contact*	*Address*	*Tel. number*

MY SOURCES

Name of organization	*Name of contact*	*Address*	*Tel. number*

MY SOURCES

Name of organization	*Name of contact*	*Address*	*Tel. number*

INDEX